THE
UNLIKELY
CANDIDATE

AN AMAZING JOURNEY OF A HEART
TRANSPLANT PATIENT

BY KELVIN V. SMITH

2012

Praise for
The Unlikely Candidate

"In this wonderful book, Kelvin Smith shares his remarkable journey and shows that physical and emotional strength as well as determination, faith and patience are the traits necessary for this "Unlikely Candidate" to survive and thrive. Kelvin's dedication to his own health, as well as to organ donation registration awareness, since his transplant, make him the "Ideal Candidate," as anyone who has come in contact with him knows."

Matthew Maurer MD
Transplant Cardiologist
Columbia University Medical Center

"Kelvin delivers a sober portrayal about what it is like to walk around with a terminal illness and then to be resurrected back to health. His story touches on how we find meaning in our lives, and how to turn adversity into spiritual growth. A must read".

Maryjane Farr MD MSc
Transplant Cardiologist
Columbia University Medical Center

"From the onset, I was hooked! *The Unlikely Candidate* reels you in. Page after page, it takes you on a roller coaster of emotions as Kelvin shows the reader the constant struggle of a life most can only imagine."

Adam Rodriguez
Actor, CSI Miami

"The Unlikely Candidate is overwhelmingly inspiring. I knew my brother was sick, but never as morbid as he describes here. He takes you down a trek of reality with a man fighting to stay alive. Highly informative on the necessary subject of organ donation."

Keith Bulluck
All Pro NFL Linebacker
2000-2012

"Kelvin's spirit and positive attitude shine through on every page of this extraordinary book."

Shari Maurer
Author- *Change of Heart*

"Kelvin shares his pain, laughter and sorrow through a compelling use of irony, humor and truth as he comes to terms with needing a transplant to survive. As a father, son, community member, he shows that the road to transplantation is "an uphill ride on roller skates" Only in this case; the only person who can save you from falling backwards towards death is an organ donor."

Helen Irving
CEO- President
New York Organ Donor Network

The Unlikely Candidate

This book is based, in part, upon actual events, persons and companies. I have changed the names and distinguishing features of the men and women in this book to protect their privacy. This book is also not intended as a substitute for the medical advice of physicians, and I have tried to recreate events, locales from my memories of them.

Cover design by William Lee of www.Leegraphix.com
Editing by Connie Anderson of Words and Deeds, Inc.
www.WordsandDeedsInc.com
Author photograph by Sheila Smith

ISBN-978-0-9882524-0-0

www.KelvinVsmithsr.com

Dedication

To my angel: I'm eternally grateful to a young man and his family from Ohio. I pledge to live life to the fullest, each day, for the both of us.

Thanks to the other recipients who like myself, try to live each day as if it were our last.

Most of all, thank you to the people who are brave and unselfish enough to be donors. Without you, there would be no me.

Table of Contents

Foreword

We all walk through life oblivious to things that go on which don't directly affect us. When my good friend told me he needed a heart transplant, I don't remember what my thoughts were. As stupid as it may sound, I guess I thought it wasn't that serious, probably because he was so matter-of-fact about it.

Now that I have read Kelvin's riveting book, and know the full story, I have been changed—with regards to listening, understanding, and reading between the lines—when someone has something important to share. I knew he was sick, but subconsciously, even knowing a new heart was required, I presumed everything would be fine. This was my man Smitt, a picture of health who didn't look sick, and who didn't sound sick on the phone.

Upon learning the full extent of his journey, a flood of emotions consumed me. I cannot fathom or remotely understand all that Kelvin dealt with from an emotional, psychological, and spiritual perspective, let alone the toll it took on his wife, kids, and loved ones. To know the fear, pain, and the suffering he endured brings about deep feelings of regret for not being there for him, but that is my issue to reconcile. We all believe that we empathize with others' plight in life, but until we know the full extent of the situation, we can't even come close to understanding. I had *no idea.*

Life is about overcoming the obstacles that are thrown in our paths, and Kelvin is an example and beacon of hope to those waiting for a second chance. I am proud to call him my friend, and lend my support in his commitment to pay it forward to all those now climbing the mountains he has conquered.

This book is monumental on two fronts. First, it snatches away the facade of ego and pride that men try to perpetrate. Keeping it real, we all have our fears, but we're just better at hiding them than women. Men possess an innate ability (or weakness) to not share their emotions or issues; we have been conditioned to believe that it isn't socially acceptable. The lesson here for all men is to let down the walls and pretenses that we erect in life in the name of manliness. Nothing brings forth revelation quite like the possibility of death.

Secondly, organ donation never crossed my mind as an option. In my ignorance, I always said, "I'm leaving with what I came with." Now that Kelvin is a flag bearer for the cause, and knowing how vital it was to him to continue residing in the land of the living, I have a newfound respect for organ donors. I'm sure every reader of this book will also. You never think about what you may need until you need it, so sign up to become an organ donor today. By GOD'S grace this could easily be our story.

We are all born with a purpose. Kelvin's angel gave him new life, for that I know he is eternally grateful. It has to be hard to know that someone had to die for you to live. However, if GOD is a staple in your life, you already fully understand it. As Kelvin's angel was possibly born for a time such as this, to save Kelvin's life, now Kelvin knows that he potentially was also born for a time such as this—to express and echo the importance of organ donation to anyone who is willing to listen.

Ezekiel 36:26 says, "I will give you a new heart and put a new spirit in you; I will remove from you your heart of stone and give you a heart of flesh." How fitting; much pun intended. Kelvin's faith has been renewed, and he is a living testimony that GOD is still in the healing business.

As tears of joy stream down my face, I give GOD the glory, and thank him for providing a second chance to my friend. We don't see each other or talk as often as we should, but his experience has changed my life. Often a man's ego won't allow us to express our emotions, but I am letting down my "man guard" in these words to follow: I want you to know that I respect you; I'm proud of you, and most importantly, I love you. I couldn't agree more—GOD is not done with you yet. Job well done, Smitt.

Seth Joyner
NFL Linebacker 1986-1999
3-time Pro Bowler
Super Bowl XXXIII Champion

Acknowledgments

How does one end up with a book of substance? It takes a lot of patience from the author, and especially those around him. For that reason, I'd like to thank my beautiful, loving wife, Nikki for dealing with all the late nights at the coffee shop where I did my writing. My terrific family, which includes my children, KJ, Devon, Jared, De'Asia and Kelsey, I thank you guys for having my back, supporting me and giving me a strong sense of purpose. The golden girls—better known as Grandma, Mom and Aunt Ruby, have been in my corner longer than anyone. Thanks Senora for being there, and also for standing in for Dad. To my brothers and best friends, Keith and Bo, you were always there when I needed you. And to all of my family and friends in New York and North Carolina, I know it was hard to comprehend all that was going on, but I'm thankful for your support.

And to all the friends, family, and co-workers who visited me during the long months I was in the hospital waiting, and then after I received my new heart. Your visits meant so much to me as you brought the outside world into my life.

Thanks to my outstanding doctors and medical staff, Dr. Stern,

Dr. Wasserman, Dr. Maurer, Dr. Farr, Dr. Stewart, Dr. Mancini, Dr. Rubin and nurse practitioners Maureen and Mary. You guys are the absolute best at what you do, and I'm grateful to have been under your care. The cath lab and the wonderful Denise who made us all feel special; I'm indebted to you for life.

I give thanks to the New York Organ Donor Network, as well as my friends at Transplant Saves Lives, for all of your support.

Thank you to the wonderful Shari, a great author, who served as a mentor during this process, and to my editor Connie Anderson, for doing a great job of keeping my words on track.

Last, and certainly not least, I thank GOD for his blessings and everlasting love.

About the Author

"Nobody can go back and start a new beginning, but anyone can start today and make a new ending."
- *Maria Robinson*

Kelvin V. Smith has been a heart transplant recipient for over four years. Today he is an inspirational speaker as a volunteer with the New York Organ Donor Network. A mentor to kids in his area, he is on the steering committee to establish a Boys and Girls Club in Ramapo, New York. He also serves on the board for Rockland Parent Child Center and Family Connections that advocates for underserved individuals and families in his hometown of Rockland County, New York. He graduated from Fayetteville State University with a degree in biology. Currently, he is a Grade 1A water treatment operator, and also a business owner. He and his wife live in Rockland, where they have raised five children.

Introduction

As I lay bloody and battered at the bottom of the concrete stairs, I instantly saw the lights above my head. Little did I know, this would become a familiar scene in the years to follow. It took me a few seconds to figure out exactly where I was. My head hurt and I tasted blood in my mouth. Why was I upside down? I soon remembered I was at work, alone as usual, and I must have blacked out. As I attempted to get to my feet, I thought, *This is certainly not the best scenario; I'll have to tell my doctor.*

Suddenly pain struck like a lightning bolt. I glanced towards the top of the stairs, and saw that my right foot dangled off the right side of my ankle like a wet noodle. I knew then I must have had a major episode with my heart, and the pacemaker that had been inserted a year earlier had either clunked out or was no longer effective. At a later date, my doctor would confirm that my heart had entered into atrial fibrillation, or a-fib for short, causing it to go into a sort of holding pattern. This resulted in no oxygen to my brain, the blackout causing me to topple backwards down twenty stairs, and crack my head on the concrete. Only GOD knows how I survived with just a broken ankle.

Either way I needed help. The only way to get it this help would be to crawl thirty yards up the stairs to the phone. I'm a gym rat, so I figured I'd be able to do it. Unfortunately, the thought of what must have happened earlier, coupled with the pain from my ankle, sapped most of my strength. I shook it off, and began to ascend the stairs, ever so carefully. Each movement was causing the bone in my ankle to come close to breaking through the skin. Like a scene out of the movie *Misery*, I was now actor James Caan, sliding gingerly across the floor. Involuntary tears rolled down my cheeks as nerves struck my dangling foot. During this ten-minute trek, I thought: *Why didn't the pacemaker do its job, or even more importantly, why didn't my doctors give me a defibrillator?* I knew I had a few heart rhythm problems, but I never expected this. I was obviously much sicker than I had realized. Eventually I made it to the phone, called my closest co-worker, and was taken to the emergency room. My severely compound fractured ankle was fixed, and days later, I got the upgrade to a defibrillator.

Death can be sudden and surprising, like a proverbial thief in the middle of the night, or it can be a long, drawn-out ordeal, similar to the pesky little chipmunk chewing away at your plants each day. I counted approximately four incidents like these when I "died" while battling congestive heart failure. By this I mean, at some point my heart stopped four times. Finally, after the miracle of a heart transplant on April 17, 2008, I was "re-born."

Worldwide, thousands of people await transplants, but never receive them, which unfortunately results in unnecessary deaths. Through the media and various other groups, the general public's awareness has heightened about the wonders of organ donation. However, the numbers are still staggeringly low. According to the New York State Organ Donor Network (NYODN), only 19 percent of the population are registered donors. On a national level, The United Network of Organ Sharing (UNOS) shows a slight increase of registered donors in recent years.

This book is geared toward getting the message out about how organ donation worked for me, and how a single donor can help save the lives of at least eight people. Although I'm not a big-time celebrity like singer Toni Braxton, who suffers from heart disease, or comedian George Lopez, or former basketball player Alonzo Mourning, who both received kidney transplants, or Michael Kutcher, brother of actor Ashton Kutcher, who received a heart transplant, I want to do all I can.

In an effort to reach masses of people, it helps to be well known, and have a topic that's intriguing or masterful in subject. But not everyone is a celebrity. Many people are like me. We don't know where, who, or what to turn to when life is an uphill struggle—and you're wearing roller skates. My story will show that I'm a regular guy, like other regular people, who suffered from a terminal illness. The irony here is the word *terminal* means *concluding*. Through the help of my unselfish organ donor and his family, it was my heart failure that was terminated—not me. Like to my surgeon who sliced my chest, sawed and cracked open my breastbone, I'm cracking myself wide open with my writing. I reveal a lot of inner things that will probably surprise some people, but in doing so I hope to inform you about this miraculous procedure.

The funny thing is, to the casual observer, I appear quite normal, but at a closer glance you'll see I'm far from that. My hands shake, and daily I take an abundance of pills to stay alive. My hips hurt, and my hair grows at an alarming rate from the medications." I know I'm not alone, and hundreds of thousands are like me. This is my story. I'm a man who like so many, did not fit the profile, but was stricken with heart disease. Death knocked on my door many times, but was told I was unavailable. And it's for these reasons, throughout this book I chose to capitalize the word GOD. For I know it was GOD and modern technology that saved me. Like an expensive steak, I've ordered this work-up to be filleted with all the spices and juices flowing abundantly out of me. I warn you that the following twists and turns are sharp, so buckle up as I take you on my incredible journey as a heart transplant patient.

Two *Words*

November 5, 2007

At the 1:33 mark, WHAM! I was knocked to a slight crouch on the dreaded elliptical machine. Two seconds later…WHAM! I slid to the floor in between other gym members. Was this it? Was this the dreaded heart attack I'd been dodging for years? I truly didn't know what was happening as I sat dumbfounded on the floor. I was too afraid to be embarrassed. Scooting backwards to rest my back against the wall, I peeked up to watch "them." "Them" were the people not like me—the normal folks I now knew I was not. The thunderstorm erupting in my chest confirmed this. The little stars before my eyes plus the tears came with extraordinary pain which caused my eyes to roll backwards as I prayed silently, "Lord, please no more!"

Then suddenly as the pain dwindled a bit, I was struck again—

but this time with clarity. Yes, I had been a heart patient for almost ten years now. My chest had been fully equipped with a defibrillator three years before, and the doctor warned me that one day it would save my life. Well, low and behold, today would be that day. I thought the doctor was a little off with his description "it would feel like a Mike Tyson blow." It was much closer to a giant stallion, which had "hee-hawed" and back-kicked me in the chest. I had received the implant in 2003, but it was now 2007 and I'd somehow forgotten about the possibility of this happening. Fortunately, the pacemaker-defibrillator combo helped reset my heart back into normal sinus rhythm, when it was needed.

But this episode led me to an obvious conclusion; I was a very sick man, some form of intervention would be needed for me to continue to live. Here I was, sitting on the floor (which was extremely poor gym etiquette I might add) listening to mostly elderly people ask me "are you alright?" This picture seemed very backwards. I mumbled to them I was okay, that it was "only" my defibrillator firing off. That statement alone was quite bizarre. I slowly rose to my feet and stood upright for a few moments before taking any steps. When you've been sick so long, you learn not to make any sudden moves, especially after an incident. This wasn't my first episode, but I prayed it would be my last, because down deep, I knew my body couldn't withstand much more.

After making it past the curious onlookers to my car, I drove to the place I desperately needed to be (Yes, I drove, which I'm sure was no doctor would have approved). The logical choice for most would have been the emergency room, but for me it was church. I needed help fast. I knew if I were to get it, I had to quickly put a call out quick! I hadn't been to church for a while, so my guilt took me only as far as the parking lot. Close enough, I thought. GOD hears you from anywhere, right? I sobbed out loud. I knew I was in a fight, but who was my foe? "Help me Lord," I cried and made my plea: "GOD, I don't know what you want me to do, but I'm ready. I'm ready to travel whatever path you choose for me. I raise my hands in surrender. I know I can't fight this battle alone and I beg for your help and mercy. . Please don't let me suffer. . I believe in you, and I know that only through you are all things possible. . Bless me Father, Amen."

I finally regained control of my emotions long enough to call my doctor's office—it was closed. Not surprisingly, I found this to be quite consistent with the type of day I was having. I simply left him a message with the specifics of my terrifying morning. The next day he called back, suggesting I come in immediately. His sense of urgency really shook me up. When I arrived at Dr. Bin's office, he was calm, and talked to me in a sort of "I told you so" manner. My pacemaker/defibrillator doctor, Dr. Bin, explained that my heart had jumped out of rhythm, and the defibrillator had done its job, shocking my heart back into rhythm and saving my life. I didn't have a problem with that. My problem was *the way* it went about saving my life. Dr. Bin explained how this was a good thing, reminding me I was a walking Intensive Care Unit (ICU) patient. I thought to myself, *if this is a good thing, then I am doomed.* He went on to say the amount of electricity that shocked me twice was extreme, but normal. Dr. Bin had a disturbing air of aloofness, but then again it was just *his job*—but this was *my life.*

Physically, I left his office, but mentally I left all my confidence in my existing heart back there. His description of my recent event made me realize the question was not: would my heart fail, but when would it happen? Crossing the Tappan Zee Bridge, I thought: Denial can be such a powerful condition. This was not new to me, but I'd been without incident for months, so I'd pretended I wasn't sick. I also had managed to block out that I had another doctor's visit which possibly would bring grim news. Suddenly, HONK, HONK, a huge truck honked at me as I veered into his lane. Not surprising, I was daydreaming again. I thought of the many years I spent creating and sculpting a perfect forgery of a healthy person. I went to the gym almost every chance I could, and called myself a "gym rat." Externally, everything appeared to be great. It's a fact some of the sickest people do everything they can to fake out others—including themselves. It can be another method of denial. Was that what I was doing? Yes—but lying on a gym floor can change all of that. Even though I now accepted how sick I was, I didn't want others to know. No person who is fighting for his life wants to throw up a white flag a second sooner than need be.

Furthermore, I had my family to think about, and there was much more I had to do. My son, KJ, and my younger brother, Keith, were on their way to becoming NFL linebackers. As a father and brother, I knew my support would be as vital to them as it would be to my younger sons Jared, Devon and daughters De'Asia and Kelsey. Also, I wanted to share many more years with my wife Nikki, so I'd embraced the "fake it 'til you make it" role, and life went on. It was quite a few years before I could no longer hide the severity of my heart illness and my obvious shortness of breath anymore.

Although I looked strong and healthy, I couldn't make my way through an entire parking lot or large area without stops/delays/pauses of some sort. The stops seemed "unnecessary" to others, but to me, they were imperative—and I knew it. I would check voice mails I didn't really have, buy newsstand items I didn't want, or use valet parking save extra steps. These tactics provided my body more specifically, my heart and lungs with the ability to catch up. I constantly felt the desperate need for more air.

I had become accustomed to visiting various doctors, but my illness had now progressed to require the care of Dr. Maxwell, a cardiologist/specialist. This particular appointment was "big" and changed my outlook with *two words*. Dr. Maxwell said them, I heard them, and leaving his office, my head went into a cloud of stillness and instant confusion. Reaching for his office door, I found myself preparing to meet the hallway as an actor coming from behind the stage curtains, except, there were no curtains. I suddenly felt very exposed. I was now carrying news in my head I could not yet process.

Were my senses playing tricks on me?

Had I really heard him say those two words…to me?

Should I go back to clarify yet again, maybe there was a mistake!

No! He'd said them. Walking down the hallway, as if it was simply an ordinary day, disguising my ill health, I waited to be alone. I got the chance in the elevator. In painfully slower-than-slow motion, my life flashed before my eyes, and I didn't understand any of it. I was so glad to be alone. I shouted to myself, " **HEART TRANSPLANT!**" and the two words pierced my soul.

What a frightening phrase. This menace was inside of me, and it doesn't get any closer than that, or any more real!

Exiting the building, my once-strong legs felt like rubber, making me a mushy piece of walking flesh. Had Dr. Maxwell handed me a clinical, verbal dagger of a death sentence that pierced my obviously malfunctioning heart? I couldn't believe my cardiologist had informed me that, not only would I need a *heart transplant,* (*someone else's heart*!) to live as I once lived, but that I would need a new heart to *live at all.* The news was inconceivable. My thoughts and emotions were scattered, my senses overlapping at lightning speed, leaving me extremely disoriented. Though I had hopes of finding strength at some point, *this* day yielded more questions than answers, and more fear than strength. This day I would not, could not be brave.

I couldn't help but wonder how I had become so ill? When did everything go horribly wrong? It wasn't so long ago that I was a walking, talking picture of perfect health, or so I thought. I tried to be positive, but all I could think was: *I'm going to die.* I pictured myself as a prisoner in a movie with other inmates shouting "dead man walking!" I wanted to wake from this horrific dream. I could not fight back the tears that welled up in my eyes. I got the feeling that the hill I had yet to climb was higher and more deadly than I could even imagine.

The 500 feet to the car seemed to take an eternity, I felt as if I was walking in quick sand. My eldest child Kelvin Jr., ("KJ") at 19-years-old, had decided to accompany me on that day. For two hours he waited patiently for his "Pops." I thought he would be asleep when I returned. But in case he wasn't, I did all I could to make myself look "normal" before reaching the car. I put four drops in my teary eyes to clear the red, cleared my throat, and adjusted my posture. It was a beautiful summer day, but the possibility existed that I would change the forecast in a quick "heartbeat" (pun intended).

I finally made it to the car and Kelvin Jr. had, in fact, been asleep. As he stirred, I hoped that he would be too groggy to talk about the appointment, but no such luck. He adjusted his seat, and asked, "How'd it go, Pops?" Inside my head I thought, "Poker face... poker face..." I wished that I could reminisce with KJ, now playing college football at Syracuse, about the last high school football game he'd played right across the street from where the car was parked. It would have been so much simpler. The fact is, as a parent, I had always prided myself on being a pillar of strength for my kids, but on this day, I felt totally weak. On this day, some level of determination and certainty in my response would have to replace true "strength," of which I had none. I said, "The game has changed, man. They're saying I'm going to need a heart transplant." Of course, I softened the blow by giving him some favorable scenarios that had been explained to me. I would never share how afraid I actually was. KJ, was a future NFL draft pick, but on this day, like any other day, he was my son. The news his "Pops'" needed a heart transplant caused KJ to sit up, looking like the four-year-old boy he once was. He was still my kid and he needed to know that I was going to be fine.

And I needed him to believe it so that he would not see my fear. Maybe, just maybe, if he could believe it, I could too.

Timing really is everything, and I knew it was, neither, the time or the place for an extended explanation of how sick I really was. True to his nickname, "Nonchalant," KJ's response to the findings was a simple, "Wow, You Cool?" For the love of my son, I lied and said "yes," and we trekked back home. There was a peculiar quietness in the car as we both tried to internally handle the future.

KJ would eventually drift off back to sleep, but unfortunately, I had to stay focused on the highway. I wanted to sleep. Actually, what I really wanted was to go to sleep and awake from this terrible nightmare. Instead, I was left alone with my own thoughts for the 40-minute ride home. After receiving bad news, the rides home, being left to deal with your projected future, are brutal. I began to realize that all the other doctors I'd previously seen, represented general medical practices, and each of them had led me closer and closer to the type of specialist that I needed.

Dr. Maxwell, specialized in cardiomyopathy (disease of the heart muscle). In my case, he had further narrowed the definition to restrictive cardiomyopathy, a stiffening of the heart muscle. How did Dr. Maxwell figure this out? Was I really comfortable taking this prognosis from a doctor who had no permanent office? The fact is, I liked and trusted him with all my "stuff." Other doctors asked me standard questions like "how many blocks can you walk?" or "how many stairs can you climb?" He knew specifically what questions to ask. I *finally* felt comfortable revealing my *extreme* shortness of breath, and told him my breathing strategies. Through deductive reasoning, my medical history file, and his own multitude of tests, Dr. Maxwell determined that my heart would one day be useless. Having heard this news made me "air out" my history of the heavy drinking, occasional drug use, and promiscuity. He assured me these were not the cause of my heart problems, which were, more than likely, genetic. This was a relief. I don't think I could have carried the guilt of knowing I was responsible for my heart's demise. That would have been too much.

Then my thoughts leaped to the great possibility of a transplant. If I was lucky enough to receive one, they lasted on average, ten years. Of course, Dr. Maxwell told me that many recipients live more than twenty years. He was a good doctor. What else was he supposed to say?

Dr. Maxwell chose to leave out some key points such as:
- The immunosuppressant medication required to keep the new heart from being rejected, might wreak havoc on my kidneys. I'd have to take it for the rest of my new life;
- I could develop avascular necrosis (death of bone tissue);
- My hands would probably always shake; and
- The very worst scenario–my body could reject the new heart, resulting in death.

No, Dr. Maxwell was a good doctor, and much too smart to bombard me with potentially damning news.

Timing is everything, and I would have time to worry about possible side effects later.

The introduction of a potential heart transplant was a hard pill to swallow, but it caused me to get my life in order. I wasn't sure about the length of time I had left on earth, but I did understand my faith in GOD would always provide a path for me either here or in the hereafter. Like the preacher always said, "Get your house in order." Living in harmony with this spiritual belief, I began to do better physically.

I became even more attentive to what I ate and drank, even though I'd always eaten well and was an athlete. I guess that's why initially I questioned, *Why me?* At this point, going to the gym was a struggle, but stopping going was simply not an option.

I worked my butt off to deflect any rumors of my debilitating health, and no one knew that, underneath my clothes was a muscular man, with one severely damaged muscle—his heart. The more unbearable my sickness grew, the more I wished I could trade in everything else for good health. I went from not believing Dr. Maxwell's theory of my needing a potential heart transplant that he had made in 2003, to falling down in a gym years later. Now it was serious. This finally made me concede that a heart transplant was indeed a reality.

My family was always important to me, but now their value was "off the charts." My children were an obvious part of my legacy, and I wanted them to see I was going to be here. I tried to make every game, every event, PTA meeting, birthday party, you name it. If my life was to be cut short, transplant or not, it was important for me to be remembered for something. I wasn't so sure about this whole heart-transplant idea, and truthfully, it left me reflecting on how I'd gotten to this point.

Please, No Lap Dance

It's the simplest things in life that we sometimes take for granted. Breathing and walking are come to mind. I grew up in the pre-Playstation era, so outdoor activities were all-day events. We kids would grab a jug of Kool-aid and some snacks in the morning giving Mom the entire day alone. In our neighborhood we'd go from football to softball to street hockey to a game called ring-o-leavio (catch me if you can). It's funny though, I never heard anyone complain about being tired and we ran from morning to night. The older we got, the more organized sports played an integral part in our growth, but they certainly didn't stop us from playing neighborhood games. After removing our uniforms, we'd jump into a neighborhood game, and play until being called in by our parents. Actually, my mom never really had to look for us because, after all, her boys were young studs who never complained about "silly" things such as health issues or being tired. We would go inside only after the rest of the kids were forced in.

Even after a doctor had examined me for a physical in the early seventies to play Little League and said that I had a heart murmur, neither Mom nor the doctor was concerned. I was a rambunctious nine-year-old. Heart murmurs were considered a general diagnosis back then, meaning it could be something very simple. In retrospect, I wonder if that doctor's analysis meant something really was going on inside my chest at the time. That's a difficult question to answer especially since my heart didn't appear broken. So why fix it? Medical technology wasn't as advanced at that point, so the dice rolled—and I went on with life. Oh yes, the rolling the dice would become a staple in my existence. Later on, I would have three hernias, appendicitis and a broken hand, but never anything associated with a heart problem.

Little League was probably the most memorable part of my childhood. I simply loved it. I was a lanky kid, so baseball was right up my alley. I loved my team, coach and teammates. This was my first lesson about camaraderie.

We were the little boys of summer, having the best time. Everything was pure, unrestricted fun. My coach always joked with me about how slowly I ran, but I never believed him because I *thought* I was running so fast. Later I found out that I was more quick than fast.

Unlike today's kids, we were physically active all the time. We ran all the time, but we never complained about being out of breath. You never heard us say, "Wait up Frankie, let me rest up for a second." I never minded running in practice because I would never tire. Aerodynamics probably enabled me to slice through the wind more efficiently since I was only about 65 pounds soaking wet.

I was also a walker. I'd walk everywhere. It didn't matter as long as there was a ball to follow. I would never tire on those memorable solitary walks to and from my games with my bat over my shoulder and my glove on my hand. As I look back, I realize I didn't have much, but I was blessed with just enough.

Those very long walks helped mold me into someone with an independent and non-selfish nature. I simply made do with the resources I had. At the time I thought I was supposed to walk everywhere. I didn't envy other kids; I didn't blame it on my folks. I had legs, and if I needed to get somewhere at that age, I walked, that is what I did. Walking enabled me to soak in my surroundings, and to appreciate the small things.

Friends and other families might drive by and blow the horn, but I was still very cool with the idea of walking because this was my "thing," Did I know deep down that some day walking would become too hard—virtually impossible for me? I dreamed of the day I would have the best car and no one would ever honk at me again. Yes, I was vain like every kid my age but I was independent as well.

When I entered high school football, I made an astonishing discovery: suddenly I hated running. I now noticed that there were a lot of faster guys. This ripped into my ego. I also took notice that I especially hated the track during practice. When that dreaded horn would blow, and coach would say, "On the track," I immediately felt like the kid from the South Park T.V. cartoon when the girl's presence made him throw up. Those three words made me nauseous as well, because I was now sixteen, and found that I could actually get tired. Looking back, maybe this was a sign of my cardiac issues. Instead of leading the pack, it took all my heart and lungs could muster to stay in the middle of my teammates.

College turned out to be a little different than I expected, with the whole sports-and-breathing issues. My athletic ability, or lack thereof, determined that I wasn't going to play college football. However I did play intramural football, softball and won a few championships along the way. I was actually debating about becoming a walk-on quarterback for the "real" football team since I was so successful on the intramural circuit. I noticed that weightlifting was helping my body mature and change. The irony is what I lacked in size, I always made up for "in heart." I didn't get tired either, but I later figured out this was because I trained at my own pace, and not a coach's stopwatch.

At the end of college, I was twenty-three-years old, and as far as I knew, I'd never had an episode of shortness of breath or anything involving my heart. Life was great. I had a college degree with a major in biology, a minor in chemistry, and a second minor in girls. I studied hard and made good grades. But I definitely played just as hard outside of my classes. I was the epitome of a healthy, successful young man with no real worries. College was a great part of my maturing process.

Life went on relatively normally, as far as my health was concerned, for about thirteen years, until I was in my mid-thirties. Then some things happened that caused distinctive shifts in my life. Life altering things like the following:

July 6, 1998 was like any other night at my four-to-midnight job at the water company—or so I thought. As I neared the end of my shift, I changed my uniform and slipped into my "hit-the-club" clothes. Earlier in the day, I had gone to the gym, gotten a fresh haircut, and had my car washed. All that was left was for the clock to strike midnight. As soon as the next shift relieved me, I was Fred Flintstone sliding down the dinosaur's back when the whistle blew. It was time, and the Friday night transformation was now official. I went from mild-mannered utility worker to "Rico Suave." I jumped into my car, and guzzled down the ice-cold beer I'd bought earlier. Next, I splashed on my expensive cologne and turned the music up extremely loud. Bopping my head to the beat, I began my trek into the city.

Frequenting strip clubs seems to be a difficult concept for many to comprehend—especially women. Of course, this is based purely on my personal survey (scantily clad dancers excluded). Strip clubs were places where people, mostly men, could drink, socialize, listen to great music, watch the game and "glance" at nearly nude women.

It's a sort of *perfect storm* for men. Afterwards, most patrons go home to their wives, girlfriends, or alone. Still, there were a few who wanted to hook up, and some did. I wasn't there for the latter, although my past track record would suggest otherwise. But here I was, back at the club, except this time minus my friend Mikey, who stood me up. It didn't matter, I thought, *why not? It is a beautiful summer evening, and I've worked hard all day, so I deserve this.* I felt healthy as an ox, and had most of my life together. By this, I mean I was at the end of a long-term relationship, but already had a new one, which left me a bit confused. I only wanted to unwind, and let my hair down.

Determined to make the most of the night, I ordered a jack and coke (sometimes called a "crack and coke" for its dizzying effect). With my back to the bar, I observed my surroundings and the diversity of the crowd. The men continuously shelled out dollar after dollar to their choice of G-string-adorned, big-breasted women. I recognized how demeaning it was for the women to show their breasts for a buck and do extra tricks for another buck. As for the men, I was somewhat sympathetic; they seemed to be very desperate to have a woman. But I realized both sexes were getting their needs fulfilled, and no laws were being broken.

An hour into my stay, I was greeted at the bar by a vivacious dancer named Carmela whom I actually recalled meeting the previous week. We talked a bit, and after a couple of drinks, I realized it was getting late. As I prepared to leave, Carmela asked if she could hitch a ride to the Bronx. Ever the nice guy, I replied "Of course!" Later I recalled how she tipped off her bartender friend with a wink when she left.

Now this is when the story gets a little weird because the next thing I knew, I was waking up in my car. I was in a daze, and soon realized I'd been in a car accident. The passenger side was smashed in, and wouldn't open. My driver's door was ajar as if someone had opened it to get in or out. *Hey wait a minute,"* I thought, *Carmela was with me, had she climbed over my unconscious body to get out?* I was able to regain my composure enough to get my car towed and find a ride home. On the way home, I thought about what type of person leaves another for dead? I was convinced something had been put into in my drink. Perhaps Carmela and bartender friend had done this before. Maybe this was a little game they played on unwary customers. Although I was only injured a bit physically, mentally I was scared because I was sure I'd been caught up in a scam. My tolerance for alcohol had always been pretty high, but this duo had a scheme going on that was almost fatal. However, except for a bruised sternum from the steering wheel, I was pretty much okay. To this day, I'm not sure if it this incident coincided with the onset of my problems—or if the accident spurred my heart troubles to begin.

This incident was significant because a month later I was in Denver, Colorado visiting a friend when I became very fatigued and short of breath. I blamed it on the altitude and my recent accident. Never, ever, would I attribute this to heart problems. While in Denver, I had my first near fainting spell. Again, I never thought it was my heart. I even blamed it on all the chicken wings I'd eaten. I searched for other reasons because I thought I was too healthy to have these issues. Upon returning to New York, I went straight to the doctor who referred me to my first cardiologist, Dr. Raines. Dr. Raines ran me through a battery of tests, including the dreaded stress test, which, if there were a grading system, I would have surely failed. I could barely complete it. I had *mitral valve prolapse,* and more surprisingly, a blocked artery. This couldn't be possible. I ate healthy food, I worked out at least four times a week, and I was two hundred plus pounds of muscle. I was Big Smitty for GOD's sake! No one would believe I had a heart problem.

This news produced opposing emotions in me. The first was sadness because I couldn't believe "I" was sick. Now my family, most importantly my kids, would look at me as "less than" their strapping, healthy dad. The second emotion was happiness, because after unblocking the artery, I was sure that both my blood flow and breathing would return to normal. As it turned out, the doctor was wrong. It was a false positive test. Terrific. I was back again to those two emotions—happy because there wasn't a blockage, but saddened because they had not yet figured out why I was short of breath. My battle against this invisible foe continued.

Life can take you on an unbelievable ride. I went from running like the wind, with not a care in the world, to becoming winded by the slightest physical activity.

The Invisible Foe

One night I dreamed I was in the midst of a fight, swinging furiously in the dark. My unseen opponent kept antagonizing me, and seemed to want to do me harm. More specifically, he wanted me DEAD. I swung and I jabbed at a spot in the darkness, hoping to maim my enemy. There was only one problem. I had no clue who or what I was fighting. "Show yourself!" I shouted. "At least have the decency to grant me that!" Eventually, I awoke from this nightmare, or did I? Like so many of us who are sick, we're not so sure what we're battling. One thing I learned early on was there is no fairness in love, war, or *sickness*.

In late April of 2007, we were all preparing for the NFL Draft in which KJ was about to be chosen. The little party of family and friends was gathered at Felicia's house, my former longtime girlfriend and KJ's mother. It was suppose to be a festive event, and one of the happiest times of KJ's life, but early on I saw a problem. There seemed to be a power struggle at this time between KJ's girlfriend and his mother, Felicia. They both meant well, but operated very differently. KJ's girlfriend, Janice, wanted to constantly be with him, offering support, while Felicia cooked, prepped, and really wanted Janice to help by running errands for the party. Felicia rejoiced in her role as usual, but always looked as though she wasn't happy. KJ called me early in the morning about the power-struggle issue, and on perhaps the biggest day in his entire life, I heard the displeasure in his voice. I told Felicia about KJ's concerns, but soon realized that trying to come between a mom and her son's girlfriend is a no-win situation. It was also about this time that I realized I wasn't feeling my absolute best.

In fact, I felt horrible. The added stress of planning the party, and then playing referee, was not helping. I couldn't believe with the multitude of blessings in my life, my heart chose this time to grow weaker. KJ was drafted in the seventh round by the Miami Dolphins, and we all cheered and embraced. Finally, all the problems became a temporary distant memory. A little later I found a quiet spot to be alone. I looked at myself in the mirror and cried, partly because I was so elated for my boy, but also because doing the actual cheering had almost caused me to faint. I could tell the excitement had almost pushed my defibrillator to the brink of firing, which it hadn't done yet. I was sick and tired of being sick and tired.

Months later, I was able to visit KJ in Miami, and help set up his living arrangements. But it was when my friend Drew and I visited in late August for a game that I began to really feel the fatigue associated with cardiac failure.

Other than seeing KJ play his first NFL game, I had no desire to leave the hotel room. I'd have Drew bring me something back to eat. Later when everyone wanted to go to South Beach, all I wanted to do was go back to the hotel and lie down. Since I loved the beach and Miami as a whole, this was quite uncharacteristic of me. I felt like the extreme party pooper, and was sure I was disappointing

Drew who didn't very often get time off from work. No one else knew—but heart failure was rearing its ugly head. It was becoming so much harder to fake it. I felt like I was finally losing this battle. Apparently, the borrowed time with my current heart was growing short.

The most ironic element about this part of my illness was the worse I felt, the more I worked. I hardly ever took a sick day, and still managed to work more overtime than anyone else at my job. I can only assume this was an inner coping mechanism. I was rationalizing that if I could make it to work, then I wasn't truly sick. The only problem was that I'd work and come home, cook, but spend the rest of the night on the couch. This continued for a month and a half. No more gym or nights out for dinner and a movie.

I felt like I was letting down my kids and wife. I simply couldn't do it. I wondered, *is my time up?* Around mid-November, the gym incident I mentioned earlier took place. I'd been determined to get back to the gym, to search for the elusive energy I once had. This was an attempt to psyche myself out, and fool my body into thinking I was simply out of shape, rather than think it was my heart shutting down. Of course, that went horribly wrong when the defibrillator fired for the first time. If I had put the progression of my declining health on a graph, the slope would have been extremely steep at this point.

December of 2007 was snowy. As a January baby, I loved the snow, but with a heart condition like I had, it took its toll. Snow, like sand, adds resistance to normal walking, so if you couple this with heavy boots and thick clothing, my breathing became treacherous. My shortness of breath was already substantial.

I was responsible for water treatment, and worked most shifts alone. I loved snowstorms, but since becoming sick, I'd begun to hate them because my job also consisted of keeping walkways clear in case of an emergency water-main break. The outside crew needed to react very quickly. I was either lifting test tubes for water testing analysis or lifting a shovel in a blizzard. With all the days and nights I worked in bad winter weather, it was bound to happen. Being stuck at work for 16 hours in whiteout conditions, during which time I had to be out in a blizzard at three a.m. risking my life, with a shovel as a deadly weapon. I'd remove two shovels full of snow; then take a quick break because my heart would be racing, and my breath would be short. I could literally see my heart beat. Of course, this would make my defibrillator stay on alert, as if to say, "Be on guard, this guy's about to croak." My walking was slow and methodical because I simply couldn't get air to my lungs. I thought of my job as a sort of safe haven, which was ludicrous because so many factors there could hasten an episode. Most of the time I worked alone, so no one got the chance to see how really sick I'd become. I was good. A walking, talking time bomb, but I was good.

Occasionally I'd work with co-workers or even worse, my boss, and we might have a particular job detail that I knew I couldn't perform. Reluctantly, I'd be forced to let the secret out that I wasn't feeling too well that day. Everyone was extremely sympathetic, especially my boss. My illness wasn't something I wanted to share, but eventually, it became so obvious it couldn't be hidden anymore. We all have worked jobs where people call in, saying they are sick, for the silliest of reasons. I'd never done that due to my heart condition, so if I complained, they knew I had a reason. That in itself was an amazing feat. Ten years with heart failure, and never took a day off because of it? Those are Cal Ripken numbers! He played baseball for almost sixteen years without ever taking a game off.

Towards the end of December, I noticed swelling in my ankles and feet. The small tree-like capillaries that were beginning to show from my poor circulation were now hidden under the swelling. After working all day, my feet would hurt, and I found myself loosening my steel-toed boots more and more each day. I eventually went to wearing only sneakers because they stretched and were more comfortable, so when the swelling came, the sneakers were easier to slip off for a quick reprieve. By the time January came, my ankles were morbidly swollen, and my doctor prescribed more Lasix pills to pull the fluid out. I hated Lasix because it really made me plan my day or travel schedule around when I took it. Lasix causes one to urinate at a furious rate, and can bring on battles of gout, which is calcium build-up in the joints. My gout episodes were mainly in my feet, making it extremely difficult and painful to walk.

I knew things were getting rough when my condition forced a change in the usual expressionless faces of my doctors. They prescribed medication upon medication, trying but failing to help my case. I assume most doctors make decent poker players but as my health was taking its final plunge, I began to see right through them. My biggest problem was I didn't know if I truly stood a chance to live. I knew the options, and for me, death was not one. Although I was so tired of this fight, I simply couldn't give up.

I was reminded of yet another cliché: "Just when you think you have it bad, someone always has it worse." My boss, Tim, suddenly died of cancer, three short months after the initial diagnosis. He never stood a chance. At least I had a heart transplant to look forward to. Right? Transplantation is a medical marvel, like sending people to the moon. But there's still no cure for cancer, I find that to be incredible. A week after my boss died, I was admitted to the hospital. As bad as I felt bad for my boss' family, I knew the possibility of my death would wreak havoc on my own family. Tim's death ignited more of a will to live. A few months earlier, he'd been the one asking me, "Was I okay," and now suddenly he was gone. He was my boss but more than that, he was my friend. Sometimes life isn't fair, and death is certainly a cheater. He wasn't even given a cap gun going into his battle. As I looked at his wife, son, daughters, grandkids and even his mother, one thing was certain: I had to fight, if not for me, then, at least, for my family. Tim was a great man, and even in his death, he gave me more reason to never complain, and to keep fighting.

Emergency Room Drama

February 2, 2008: I was startled when I woke up on the bathroom floor—and didn't know why! In addition, my lip was bloody, my head had a knot the size of an egg, and I had lost control of my bowels. I was completely disoriented, and had no idea what had happened. I regained my composure, eased down the stairs, and alerted my wife, asking her to please run a shower. Out of consideration for her need for some sleep, we were temporarily sleeping in different beds on different floors—due to my all-night, severe congestion, wheezing, coughing, twisting, tossing, and turning.

Being the concerned wife, she should have been able to safely assume that after "the bathroom incident," a trip to the emergency room would follow. Not so. The reason was obvious: long-term New York NFL fans *prefer* not to miss Super Bowl Sunday games when the NY Giants are playing. Being the proud fool, I thought it could wait until *Monday,* rationalizing that the worst was probably over anyway. I was alive, albeit barely, and even tried to take over the kitchen to make my famous hot wings, but…I couldn't. My mind said yes but my body screamed no. After Nikki set me up on the pullout couch, I coached her on how to make them. My body felt even *worse* than the gym episode three months earlier. I felt about five times worse than the time I had the car accident that broke my sternum a while back. So…we watched the game, but…the wings… and the beer…tasted different. I tried to act as if everything was the same, but it was a far cry from previous Super Bowl Sundays. There was no crowded house, no loud screaming and no side bets. In fact the only safe bet was that my health was going to get worse before it got better.

I was convinced the end was drawing closer. On this special Sunday, the New York Giants won the Super Bowl, and New York was in for a major party. As I coughed my head off, I couldn't have cared less. Tuesday came, and I still had not moved off the pullout couch. I took cough medicine and watched the ticker tape parade on TV. Any attempts to stand on my feet would swell my ankles so badly, that I would boomerang right back to the couch. I tried to get some sleep in between the coughing spells, but the congestion me feel as if I was drowning inside.

Nikki took a half-day off from work to drive me to see my pacemaker/defibrillator doctor for my three o'clock Tuesday appointment. Although I was extremely concerned with my latest incident, I figured they'd give me something—more medicines or a new apparatus in my body. Dr. Bin hit us with some disconcerting news, to say the least. This was not good. "Alarming" was a better word to describe it. After analyzing the readings, it was determined the defibrillator had pretty much *expired.* Expired? This was the unit that brought me back from death's door countless times, and now I was being told it no longer worked? The defibrillator had become my security blanket. Dr. Bin informed us that based on the results;

the unit had fired off the maximum amount of times. It was done! It had served its purpose, and similar to the other heart medications, it was time for another remedy.

The reason my body felt like a "train wreck" was because of the massive voltage that had been expended by the defibrillator. However, Dr. Bin couldn't explain why *after 45 seconds, I woke up after passing out from the arrhythmia.*

Temporarily, I took charge of the conversation. I explained to *him* not to worry because if the medical explanation was perplexing, I had my own theory: I was of the opinion that medical science is based on human knowledge, and with no disrespect to him, I told Dr. Bin it was okay if we didn't agree. It was evident to me that after the defibrillator had exhausted itself and I passed out in the bathroom, it was GOD who lifted me off the floor. Again, GOD was not done with me yet. It wasn't my time. Seeing how serious I was, Dr. Bin nodded his head as if in agreement. The one thing we definitely agreed upon was the fact that I needed immediate medical attention because my body had reached a new low. My life seemed to be passing in front of my eyes, and was a bit of a blur. Things were happening so fast I had no time to be afraid. Dr. Bin called my cardiologist, Dr. Maxwell, who in turn notified the hospital emergency room that I was on my way—and I was.

Nikki and I didn't talk very much on our thirty-minute drive to the emergency room. We were too engulfed in our thoughts after meeting with Dr. Bin. It was so surreal. I felt a quiet desperation, making a grown man entertain magical thinking; wishing real hard (almost crossing my fingers) and praying that at any moment, the alarm clock would go off, and it would be time for school. I glanced at Nikki as I drove. (Yes, I drove, somehow conscious of the possibility this might be my last drive for some time). I was sure my new bride hadn't envisioned our life together to take such a drastic turn.

We'd met in 1997, but I didn't begin to get sick until that following year. I kept her in the dark until returning from that infamous Denver trip in 1998. At that point, we were more close friends than an actual couple, and I didn't feel it was necessary to drop my "stuff" in her lap. The closer we became, the more I told her. She convinced me she was in it for the long haul. I honestly didn't know I would get sick this quickly, and relied on the possibility of my heart mending itself. I proposed to her Thanksgiving weekend in 2004. She was happy, and we knew we would now tackle any obstacle together forever. I prayed Nikki didn't feel tricked or bamboozled. Lord knows I wanted to spend the rest of my life with her. On this particular ride, I daydreamed yet once again, making a mental journey back to Jamaica and our wedding day.

The sign read, "Welcome to Ocho Rios," or better yet, paradise. We had ninety of our closest friends and family with us and Nikki was in her glory. I embraced this moment myself because the time had finally come to complete my life with my soul mate. Although we'd both loved before, we agreed this time was the right time. Months prior, we both dieted and worked out very hard in preparation for the big day. I'm sure this is what a lot of couples do prior to their wedding. She of course looked fabulous. Her wedding dress fit very snug, and she achieved her flat stomach from all of her cardio work. I looked as good as I could, considering what I was going through. These days, I was dealing with a certain insecurity about myself, especially my body and the pacemaker. Defibrillator cuts on my chest didn't help. Furthermore the defibrillator protruded and caused more attention, or so I thought. I'm a "pool-over-beach" sort of guy, but this changed since to it was less crowded on the beach than at the resort pools. However, the beach added more stress on my heart since walking through the sand was more taxing.

Still, I made sure I did everything Jamaica had to offer because in a very remote part of my mind, I wasn't sure if I'd ever make it back to the island. Of course, mentally I've travelled back many times. All-inclusive vacations meant a few hundred gallons of Red Stripe Beer and pounds of salty food. None of these things were conducive to my health, but I disregarded doctor's orders this once. Jet skis and other water sports would test the limits of my already-weak heart. Not all ninety of our guests knew about my heart condition. "Fake it 'till you make it, remember?"

The ceremony was terrific with only a couple of complaints by me—about me. Walking hand in hand on the beach for the photographer wore me out. Lifting my new bride took my breath away as I strained to hold her up while the picture was taken.

I felt bad because Nikki loved to dance, and I was only able to give her our first one. I recalled other weddings when the happy couple danced the night away, but I had no energy. I felt as though I was letting her down. Later at the reception boat ride, she and all of our guests did dance until their hearts were content so that helped. Above us, the moon shone brightly as I sipped my drink in the corner, and although I was sad about not being able to be out there "shaking a leg," I was happy to be alive to share so much joy with Nikki and the rest of our family and friends.

My tears began to well as I looked over at my grandmother who was totally absorbed in all the festivities. As the boat swayed back and forth, she sat still in her wheelchair. Earlier in the evening, four strapping guys had carried her in that wheelchair across the sandy beach. It was a terrific sight to see her look like a true queen as she was being carried around. I could only watch while wishing I was one of the men who carried her aloft. The amount of strength and breath necessary would have certainly set off my defibrillator, changing the complexion of our wedding night—altogether.

But everyone was happy. My sons and daughters were ecstatic, and coupled with Nikki's joy, this was a momentous time. Not only was my bride beautiful, but her body language told me she had not a care in the world. It was the first time in my life I truly believed I made everyone around me proud. The funny thing: for a little while, I actually forgot I was battling for my life.

Reluctantly I snapped back to the present moment. I glanced over at Nikki who had a different type of aura now. For all of her happiness on our wedding day had now shifted into fear of the unknown. We continued our solemn drive to the hospital, arriving at the E.R. at about five p.m. Though I had been in the hospital many times before, this was the first time the doctor recommended an emergency room for "immediate" medical attention. We had no time to think; we simply reacted to the prompts. These were unchartered waters, and I certainly wasn't the captain of this ship. I was going along for a ride on the rough, dark sea, and we really didn't know what to expect.

Some medical personnel awaited our arrival, and with them was my cardiologist, Dr. Maxwell. He explained they were trying to get me a bed upstairs as soon as possible, but the process could take an unusually long time. I wasn't really altogether clear about what he meant by that. When I finally got done with the tedious paperwork, it was time to move through the emergency room doors. What I found on the other side was unbelievable. It looked like I imagined a wartime medic unit in Vietnam. This had to come close. People from all walks of life were waiting for various types of help for every kind of illness. Tubes and IVs were everywhere. Patients were crammed in every nook and cranny of the ER. It was a sight to behold.

Since not everyone was waiting to be admitted, I knew I'd be waiting a while. I didn't glance at the clock until around 8:00 p.m. Nothing was happening. Around me I heard audible sighs of frustrations, almost everyone had an attitude, and seemed upset about having to wait so long. Suddenly, as if this newfound experience had not been "fun" enough, and someone had to "add spice" to this incredible boredom, in walked the *IV nurse*.

I had always been told how great my veins were. However, this nurse couldn't quite seem to *find* one? She simply couldn't pierce *one,* or at least not the *right* one? So, before she caused me to "bleed out," she had the sense to call another nurse for help. Thankfully, the second IV nurse knew what she was doing, came in and got it on the first try. As if not wanting to belittle her co-worker, the second IV nurse smiled and shook her head. Underneath her breath, she murmured to me "Nice veins." If ever there was an E.R. superhero, she was one for me that day. That was procedure number one—a prelude to many. I was later thankful that this (sometimes painful) procedure had to be re-done only every five days or so.

The lethargic and slow motion of the E.R. was a concerning paradoxical mess. It was an emergency room, but no one seemed to be in a rush. As I looked over at an older gentleman with a bandaged head, and noticed that it was now 10:00 p.m., I joked to Nikki, "How old was he when he initially arrived?" It was tough to keep a sense of humor, but I promised myself I would—or die trying.

In the E.R., there was so much *"nothing"* going on that the staleness in the air seemed to rob our collective thoughts. Maybe that's why we all decided it was better to have an attitude about the "wait" than to think about why we were really there. The bad news came so fast.

We saw the doctor at three p.m. and at five p.m. I'm here in the E.R.? Maybe I tried to distract myself; maybe I tried NOT to think. Maybe, in the absence of certainty, numbness feels better, takes less energy, and makes more sense. How could I make peace with the thoughts with which I was grappling? The fact was: the defibrillator that I carried in my chest that worked so hard trying to convert my heart back into rhythm—and had saved my life a few times—had now stopped working. Similar to the day at the gym when it went off and saved my life, I leaned on my Savior. Again I asked for GOD's help. In this instance, I simply wanted to take a good, clean breath as I waited in this hellhole of an E.R.

I had heard that GOD *always* answered prayers, and that the answers are always answered in one of three ways: 1) Yes, 2) No, or 3) Wait a while. Maybe I would have wondered if that was true. Maybe I would have wondered if, instead of calling myself a "proud fool" a few days ago on Super Bowl Sunday, after the "bathroom incident," I would have given myself a little credit for recognizing the indications that there was a significant shift in my life, and something wasn't right. I may have wondered from Sunday to Tuesday: 1) If I was gliding by on GOD's mercy and His borrowed breath 2) How many times angels, one on each side of me, were doing the job of the "out-of-order" defibrillator 3) My instincts knew that leaving home would change my life forever, and that's why I knew that, as counter-intuitive as it seemed, I had hung onto my home for a little while longer.

At some point, I had to give a urine sample, and the bathroom had a smell I'll never, ever get out of my head! I literally almost threw up; it smelled like feces, urine and death. Although I was in the hospital, I didn't feel comfortable in the E.R. I truly felt like this was a place where I could get even sicker. Thankfully, about one that morning, my number came up, a room was available…finally.

Okay, Huddle Up

At 1:30 A.M. I arrived on the fifth floor South Greenery. I didn't realize it at the time, but this would be my home for almost three months, and luckily for me, this wing had some of the nicest employees on earth, beginning with the lead receptionist. Mrs. Tyson was an older, Jamaican woman a few months short of retiring after thirty years of service. I was really glad to get into a single room. Not that there is anything wrong with a double room, but I really appreciated my privacy, and it gave me less chance of contracting someone else's illness. My health was bad enough so if my roommate had a virus or any other infection, it could possibly compound my already existing major problems. Other than my doctors, Mrs. Tyson was the first health professional to show that she really cared. She came to my room and explained how insurance companies and hospitals work. In a few words, she explained the first lesson that if you didn't ask for extras, then you certainly wouldn't be given them.

My plan was simple. I wasn't going to make any waves, and I definitely wasn't going to piss off the hospital employees. I saw it similar to being at a restaurant, always making a fuss and sending your food back, only to have it return with fresh spit (or so the stories go). Oh no, I wasn't going to be the patient who complained continuously—the one who, when he did take a turn for the worse—caused the nurses to take their time answering the call bell. I felt indebted to Mrs. Tyson who extended herself. She even had both of her sons come to the hospital to meet me.

Mrs. Tyson was great, and she reminded me of my mentor— my grandmother. Alma Smith was the matriarch of my family, and was responsible in many ways for the type of person I am. She instilled in me all that was good, and is undoubtedly one of the main inspirations for this book. Always the one sacrificing, always working two or three jobs to make sure her two daughters and grandkids were okay, my grandmother was my hero. Grandma was always looked at as "diesel," meaning she was strong and powerful. There was nothing that she couldn't do, and she took absolutely no grief from anyone. My grandmother scared me more than any man, including my father. If you did something wrong, she would beat the hell out of you, but if you did right, she would smother you with undying affection. It wasn't so much what she said that affected me, it was what she did. Her work ethic was impeccable. The way she cooked was unbelievable. It was her whole "me-last" attitude that really stood out. All of those things groomed me from a boy into a man. She was, and still is, my idol.

Until she had a stroke a few years ago, Grandma could run circles around everyone. When I was having breathing problems, she would actually be doing laps around me in the airport—because that's what she did. When she got sick and had a stroke, I was really destroyed. Word reached me on my way to Hawaii. Imagine that, on my way to paradise, my hero had a stroke. My aunt was trying to keep my trip in a positive light, so she told me it wasn't that bad. When I first saw Grandma after the stroke, it ripped me apart. Suddenly the strongest person I knew was reduced to an old woman in a recliner, her speech and ability to walk were severely affected. I tried to be strong but I was devastated. My illness, which was also getting worse by now, became secondary. It was hard for me to function, let alone leave her and go back to my life—but I had to trust her doctors, and first and foremost, trust GOD.

About a year had passed after the stroke, she was getting better, but I was getting worse. Still nobody truly knew how bad it was because it was my nature to protect my family, I didn't want them to be afraid for me. In April 2005, we all went to Tennessee for my brother's celebrity basketball tournament, and my grandmother got sick again. I still get chills when I think about the way my mom called my name throughout the stadium to come help Grandma. When I got to her, it was a sight I'll never ever forget. Her eyes looked dead, like that of a great white shark. Piercing through me, they were saying "Help me Kelvin, please help me!" I felt helpless, like a total imbecile. How could I not know that she was having a diabetic reaction? Fortunately, again she came through. I was determined to never feel helpless like this again. I researched her condition, and prepared myself for the next potential event.

Due to a small hole in her heart, Grandma would have to get a pacemaker, a device with which I was very familiar. She kept regaining her health, only to have another setback. I made a vow to stay closer. The more episodes I had with my health, the more I knew it would really bother my grandmother not to be able to be by my side like she always had been. Subconsciously, I nominated Mrs. Tyson as my honorary grandmother. Alma Smith always gave me strength, and I looked to Mrs. Tyson to fill that void.

Another great individual, Nurse Ann, helped me settle into my room. Ann was beautiful inside and out, and answered any, and all, questions my wife or I had. One of first questions was, "Kelvin, have you been listed?" At that time, new to everything, I really didn't understand, but Ann explained that she wondered if I'd been listed for a heart transplant yet? She said that there were different levels of listing, depending on how bad one's condition was. She added, "All of these things will be cleared up later by Dr. Maxwell."

My room was small, yellow and had an oversized clock with a loud ticking you couldn't miss at night. I had a standard hospital bed, but the nurse was able to extend the length a bit to accommodate my 6'1" height. My small flat screen TV swiveled over the bed. I had a great bathroom, except I couldn't use the shower, and there was no hot water. The hospital had a bacteria thing going on, and insisted that all patients drink bottled water, using it for brushing teeth and washing your face.

But perhaps the best or worst feature, depending on my feeling on any given day, was my view out the window. Five stories above the front entrance of the hospital, it would become my daily virtual tour of the outside world. The busy street with the hustle and bustle of New York traffic and pedestrians became my live TV. Although I came in during the dead of winter with snow falling, someone told me that my window faced the garden across the street. Currently, it was difficult to imagine a plush green garden. They told me I'd be able to watch the beautiful flowers bloom in the spring. At the time, I scoffed at the idea of still being here to see them. I could see the hotdog street vendor from whom I purchased my last two sodium-filled franks before going on my severely reduced sodium diet. I started to wonder if maybe I'd been strategically placed in this room to be tortured to death. I missed a good hot dog. I was determined to one day visit that hot dog vendor again, but first I had a whole lot of work to do to get better, and my plan was to stick to my doctor's script. Finally I was in a place where I didn't have to feel so afraid anymore, so after analyzing my situation, and getting acclimated to my new surroundings, I sent Nikki home. She needed to get some rest, and I knew I was going to need her. I told her to go home and not to worry because I was safe, and would be right here later that day. Reluctantly she obliged, leaving me to my new home and returning to our old one.

Spending nights at the hospital was a new phenomenon with all the smells, bells and whistles, which took some time to get used to. Getting rest in the hospital was really not an option—there was just too much going on. Even my very first morning consisted of various tests and prodding. Blood pressures and blood tests were done very early. Medicines were consistently administered through my IV, and I was given a Holter monitor, which was hung around my neck, constantly checking my heart rate. It was the size of an ice tray, and was programmed to alert the nurses at the front desk after it sent a signal across the street to its network base. Any sudden change in my heart rate caused nurses to come running. This little apparatus became pretty nerve-racking since false alarms regularly sent a nurse to my room to check on me. As I lay still in my bed watching TV, I'd simply reply that I was okay. It's not as if I was watching a scary movie or anything that would cause a certain change, but I came to grips with the fact that my heart was very weak—and it did what it wanted. The nurses made sure I didn't "check out of life," at least not on their shift. Seriously though, the vast majority of professional people at the hospital were dedicated employees who seemed to put the patient first.

As with all jobs, occasionally there are a few exceptions to the rule, the employee who basically does the bare minimum. Fortunately, I didn't have to interact with many of them. When I did come across a particular worker like such, I'd make it extremely difficult by killing them with kindness. I was determined to live by the rule that it takes fewer muscles to smile than to frown. Furthermore, by nature I was an upbeat person, and just because I was confined to a hospital bed, did not mean I wasn't going to do my best to stay that way. When KJ was born, I had made up my mind to try handling most situations like I would want him or my other children to handle them. I was fighting something much bigger than a disgruntled employee, and I was only passing through the hospital, while they had to continue to work there. Life in general was short, and being sick in the hospital made it seem possibly shorter. Why expend vital energy combating someone negative. The bigger picture made me realize these were, indeed, small potatoes.

Later the first day, Dr. Maxwell came in to explain the whole whirlwind I was going through. In the last few days, my life had changed drastically. It was always a relief to see my doctor, especially now because I had no idea what I was really up against. As nice as my new nurses were, they were still strangers. Dr. Maxwell was not. He was like a friend, and although I knew he didn't always have the best news, at least he was painfully honest. Today would be no exception. He sat on the edge of my bed and began to explain my options. He started by saying that my heart was getting weaker and simply couldn't keep up with the rest of my body's demands for blood. It was a domino effect. My bad heart was starving my other organs: my liver, lungs, and brain. Now I had I clearer understanding of the jaundice in my eyes, my shortness of breath, and my lack of balance. The low ejection fraction (EF)—the heart's inability to pump blood, was what caused my defibrillator went off during the recent episodes. Up to this point, the defibrillator had been doing its job, and was saving my life, but now, for reasons the doctor couldn't explain, it hadn't bring me out of my arrhythmia attack in the bathroom that morning.

That reason, coupled with my body becoming congested and full of fluid, was why Dr. Maxell and Dr. Bin felt it was necessary to admit me. He saved the big news for last. Although he'd mentioned a heart transplant before, this time he said it much more empathetically. He said it was time to give me back my life, and again he stated that because I'd been dealing with heart disease for ten plus years, I had no idea how bad I really felt. I had become accustomed to dealing with all the adjustments necessary to accommodate for my illness. He told me my body had compensated for my bad heart, and I had simply adapted to my "new normal." The inevitable was here: I needed a heart transplant. The only other option was to leave the hospital, and take another chance with my bad ticker. He made it clear that things had gotten worse, and the time to act was now, while my only health problem was a bad heart. I didn't think Dr. Maxwell was crazy, only the news. My eyes began to tear up. I really had no words; for once I was totally speechless. Dr. Maxwell said he'd come back later because he knew it was a lot to absorb. I needed time alone. What I needed more was to wake the hell up from this nightmare. This couldn't be happening to me. I was only human. It was natural to question: *Why me?*

- Had I wronged so many folks in my earlier life that this was karma?
- Or had I had broken so many hearts that I now actually needed a new one myself?
- Was I being an idiot, overanalyzing as usual, was it simply a situation that I was born with that finally needed fixing?

I chose the latter, and began to get my head on straight. I knew GOD was my Savior and He would see me through this, like He had so many other situations. I had already surrendered my fate to Him, and was ready to accept whatever He had in store. Now, the hard part was to tell my family.

The first order of importance was to get the excess fluid out of my body. Prior to the hospital stay, I'd taken 160mg of Lasix orally, causing me to urinate unbelievably often. But now it was administered through my IV, making it much more effective and fast acting. Perhaps it was too fast because in three days I went from 205 to 163 pounds. The sudden weight and water loss caused the most severe cramping ever. I could actually watch the spasms develop in my body, like a scene from "The Mummy" movie when big bugs were under the actor's skin. It was horrible. Because the fluid was attacked so vigorously, it caused an electrolyte imbalance in my body affecting my potassium level. In turn, this made my fingers, neck, feet, legs, and stomach cramp uncontrollably, bringing me to tears. The doctors were concerned, it seemed like maybe it was done too fast. The fact that I kept producing urine was amazing to me. Fortunately I finally achieved what they called a "dry state."

I was taken off the Lasix for a while, to allow the chemicals to rebalance, but afterwards I became a stick figure. My old weight was really a false weight because it was forty extra pounds of fluid. My congestion ended, and after the cramping ceased, I was finally able to sleep at night. It was amazing how much better I felt without all the fluid. My feet and ankles didn't swell as much, and I had little or no coughing. I became so skinny that when I walked, it felt like I was floating. Since the doctors were happy with the results, I acted like I was as well. Sure, I was happy to feel better but I looked like a skeleton. I really looked sick. Before, I could get away with faking it but not now. If this was the new me, it was going to take some adjusting.

After about a week, I gathered my family in my room, to tell them I needed a heart transplant. Nikki of course, already knew. She was told as soon as the news broke, and she was on board, as usual. She had ridden this far so I knew she would handle the decision well, and she showed no fear or concerns since Dr. Maxwell had extensively explained my situation. Bo, Keith, KJ, Jared and Nikki were all in the room as the doctor explained my heart disease from past to present, touching on things that my family had no clue I'd been going through for the past ten years.

After he finished, I looked around the room to examine the guys' expressions. Nikki actually left the room to give us alone time since she had already been briefed. Out of the four, I think KJ's face showed the most concern. The older he got, the more family-oriented he was becoming. My younger brothers, Bo and Keith, took strength from each other and kept their poker faces. My youngest son Jared, age 17, was calm as well, and I tried very hard to keep my emotions in check for him. To this day I'm still not sure if they know how organ transplantation had become such a medical revelation or how lucky one has to be to receive an organ.

Dr. Maxwell then opened the floor for questions. Keith went first, asking if I be able to have my own room for my entire stay. Dr. Maxwell said that probably yes, my insurance would handle it. Keith replied, "Is that probably, or can we make that definite?" He wanted me to be comfortable, and have the best. That was the mindset of my millionaire football-playing brother though. He was a "check cutter." Dr. Maxwell smiled and said he understood, adding, "Yes, that can definitely happen." On a side note: we checked upstairs where former President Bill Clinton and former New York Mayor David Dinkins had been. Their rooms, or suites, were carpeted, had big, flat screen TVs, and two bathrooms. The cost was about thirty thousand dollars a month. Keith eventually asked me, "Do you really need ALL of that? I mean, it can be done." I politely chuckled and said, "Nah, I'm cool." This made me realize my rich brother did in fact have a financial cap. Bo went next, being a man of few words, he said, "Hey, you gotta do what you gotta do." The kids actually shocked me because they were alert and responsive. KJ's take was that it was time because he was tired of watching me suffer—and if this was the best option, then he was ready. He questioned the potential wait time for the transplant. Jared spoke next, asking, "What is the success rate of heart transplants, and how many years can my dad live with a new heart?" I was totally caught off guard because I suddenly realized that my little boy was definitely growing up. I was really proud that he asked key questions and didn't remain silent. Dr. Maxwell answered all the questions to everyone's satisfaction.

Now as a family we were all on the same page. It was an unfortunate situation, and the battle would be long and tenuous, but it was something that certainly we could conquer—together. Although the brunt of the work would be by me, my family's support would be an integral part of overcoming the odds of getting and surviving a heart transplant.

Making 6 New Friends

As the new kid on the block, nurses would ask me questions pertaining to my transplant status—and I didn't know the answers. Yes, Mr. Smith in room 212 was a rookie. Soon, though, I would lose my rookie status. I would learn everything I needed to know about the process and have the necessary information for everyone who entered my room.

When I first began my hospital stay, I wasn't on the transplant list. But I learned all the doctors and department heads had weekly meetings. One thing on the agenda was to determine which patients got listed for transplant.

The major contributing factors to get on this list were:
1. Necessity, or how bad you needed it,
2. How long you'd been waiting, our age (65 was the usual cut-off point),
3. Size and blood type, and
4. Your overall health.

I had been told that I was a prime candidate for transplant because, other than having a failing heart, I was in very good shape. I didn't smoke and only drank casually. All my other markers were also great. Initially I didn't understand why they were such a big deal, but through further education, it became real apparent. Psychologists, psychiatrists and social workers all came and interviewed me to make sure that I was in fact a good choice to be an organ recipient. Eventually it did make sense because if a person or family decides to donate organs, it is important that health professionals find a viable recipient for this heart. It is, indeed, the gift of life, and someone has to die in order for others to live. Becoming a donor is extremely noble and unselfish, so it is vital that great structure and guidelines are followed so respectful choices are made.

The structure stands firm, and is never breeched. Even former Vice President Dick Cheney had to wait like the rest of us, and didn't receive a heart transplant until age 71. He battled heart disease for 25 years, and stayed on the transplant list for two years prior to receiving a heart from an unnamed source. It doesn't matter who you are, how much money you have, your race, creed or color. The Cheney example dispelled all the rumors of favoritism I had heard of being allowed to "jump" the list. Everyone abides by the same set of rules. Strict criteria are universally followed.

Obviously I was a good choice because on February 19, 2008, I was told that I'd been chosen to be on the heart transplant list as a 1A-status patient. I was congratulated, but truth be told, I wasn't sure if I was blissful or dejected. This decision meant it was official. My chest would be sawed; cracked open, my heart taken out, and then another heart from a brain-dead person would be put into my body in order for me to live. *Live* being the keyword, if in fact I made it to that point.

Your status was of utmost importance on the hospital wing where I resided. It didn't matter who you were or the amount of money you had. Your status was strictly determined by how sick you were and where you were located on the transplant list. The listing was as follows:

- *Status 2*–the healthiest patients who are usually allowed to go home.
- *Status 1B*–patient waits at home or at the hospital, but is in the end stage of heart disease.
- *Status 1A*–patient has the most serious degree of illness, and usually waits in the hospital. (*Status 1A* patients have the highest priority).

My wing of the hospital consisted of mainly heart patients, some of whom had already had transplants years before. Some were back in the hospital because their body was rejecting their heart, and they had to be given acute medications to stabilize them. We, the current "on-deck" heart patients, were in bad shape, some more than others. As we passed each other in the hall or in the patient's lounge, the conversation usually began with, "Hi, how are you, and what's your status?" I quickly realized that if someone had a higher status, and was closer to getting a heart, then others were a little envious, which I guess is human nature. Despite this, there was a natural fraternity among us because we all had the same apprehension—the same challenging mountain to climb. There was Mr. Rich, an older gentleman about 60-years-old, with grown children, who like me had battled heart disease for years, and was an avid weightlifter. We shared many things in common, and became quite close. B.J. was a young 20-something-year-old physical education teacher whose health had taken a sudden turn for the worse. Mr. Raj, a 50-year-old man from upstate New York, was a pharmacist and extremely smart, but you could see major concern on his face. Then there was my immediate neighbor, Kayla, a 25-year-old woman who gave the nurses and doctors a hard time. Her fear and frustration from being extremely sick for so long had simply gotten the best of her.

We were all hospitalized for pretty much the same thing, but with various causes. Heart disease doesn't discriminate, as I could see from the wide assortment of patients. It was easy to bond with one another because when you saw one person walking gingerly down the hall holding a pole with two or three medicine drips flowing into his arm, it was natural to gravitate toward him. Obviously, I too had my own drips and pole, so I quickly blended into my new "family." At different times we all passed each other on the way to scheduled procedures, such as echocardiograms (ECG) or pulmonary tests. Some nights I'd hear Kayla battling extremely bad congestion, and I'd feel so sorry for her because I recalled my own battles. I might walk by Mr. Rich's room, hoping to have a conversation with him, but instead a slew of doctors and nurses would be in there because he'd had a diabetic episode. Another time he'd tell me he came by my "house," but my door was closed because I felt extremely tired that day. We were all one, big family of misfits who understood each other's woes, aches and pains. We were all fighting things that normal people couldn't fathom, but we recognized as our way of life. Being in this fight made us realize how precious life is, and how we all take it for granted. We watched out for each other. If someone was missing, we asked the nurses or doctors for updates. We were determined to beat heart failure, get back into the mainstream of society, and live as normally as possible.

As potential heart transplant patients, we all shared things in common, like low-sodium, low-fat diets. I can't really say the hospital food was bad, but if you were there to gain weight, you definitely had made a wrong turn. We were always starving (maybe not starving, but excessively hungry). Every so often, the dietician would come by and question everyone about the quality of his meals. I'd answer, "Yes, but I always find myself still a bit hungry." Usually her reply would be that the portions were made specifically for each person, but if I wanted to, I could order extra or substitute one item for another, more substantial option. I chose to not rock the boat because if she was the professional, she was supposed to know what was best for each patient. Right? Wrong! Why was it that all of us were so doggone hungry then? It got to the point where my growling stomach would interrupt any attempt I made to take a nap. Jokingly, I thought that starvation might take me out before my heart disease did. We all shared our various ways to supplement our diets. I found out that there was a restaurant upstairs that I could order from for a small fee, of course. The food was much better, and the portions were much larger, but it was eventually outgrew my budget—so that didn't last too long. Something had to give, so after speaking with my doctor, he gave me permission to occasionally get outside food.

To my surprise, everyone was already getting supplemental foods brought in. Obviously, I was the rookie and hadn't yet learned the ropes. Always a relatively decent eater, I usually prepared my food at home. Now I found it necessary to go outside the box. As if she didn't have enough to do, Nikki had yet another task. After watching me for years, she had a basic knowledge of how I ate. Nikki started to bring in extra food.

I did my best not to overdo it until Kayla walked over to my room and offered me some carrot cake. Then she and her husband told me about a BBQ restaurant and a bakery around the corner. I'd never been a real big fan of sweets but barbecued chicken, now that *was* a favorite. Although I actually wasn't malnourished, I felt like it. Many evenings that BBQ restaurant would be Nikki's first stop. I tried to trick my mind by taking the skin off, which is hilarious because at 163 pounds, I was still watching my fat intake. I also tried to rationalize that most of the seasoning or salt would be in the skin. I selfishly thought that I really didn't care if other patients ate badly because in my mind I was way ahead of the curve. But sometimes I found eating outside food was not the best thing to do. I could tell immediately if I had too much because my ankles would quickly balloon to enormous size, and I'd have this feeling of fullness around my liver.

However, my biggest deterrent was Kayla. After many conversations with her husband Joe, I realized that she did and ate what she wanted. Many nights as we all tried to go to sleep, she'd have coughing fits because she couldn't get the congestion out of her chest. I felt sorry for her because I'd been there so many times. Joe would tell me that she had eaten very poorly and was now paying for it. I saw the frustration on his face because although he tried to get her to be more diligent, she clearly danced to the beat of her own drum.

Listening to Kayla's bouts and episodes, and witnessing her frequent trips to the ICU due to her defibrillator firing, discouraged me from shirking my dietary responsibilities. All of these things scared me straight, and made me more disciplined in my preparation for the transplant. A heart transplant is a life-changing process. Approximately 2,300 transplants are done in the U.S per year, with another 3,100 people on the waiting list. The mere thought was inundating, consuming, nerve-wracking and downright scary. I was a grown man who cried himself to sleep many nights in a hospital room all alone, truly not knowing what to expect of the future—or if he had one. I felt GOD would see me through, but I knew it was normal to be concerned about the procedure and life thereafter. Just because something seems normal doesn't make it any less frightening.

On one particular morning about three weeks into my hospital stay, I made my usual walk down to the lounge so housekeeping could clean my room. I ran into a new face, Hal, a 58-year-old barber from Long Island. We struck up a conversation, and he told me he had had a transplant about twelve years ago. I was amazed because he looked terrific and extremely normal. He told me he was admitted because he was feeling sluggish, and they found that he was having a form of rejection. He was so calm, but he explained this was all part of the deal, and that it was normal. The doctors would simply bring him in and give him extra steroids through his IV. As we talked, he took a phone call from his wife, and placed a lunch order with her. I was shocked at what I heard. He told her to bring him an Italian combo hero. I said, "Wow, you can eat an Italian combo?" he replied, "Sure, basically, you can eat normally as long as you don't overdo it."

Hal became my new mentor, explaining the ins and outs of the procedure, as well as life after transplant. He gave me even more hope—to this day, Hal is one of the reasons why I make myself available to other patients. When you don't know what monster you're fighting, you don't know what weapons to bring. But after speaking to Hal who'd fought and won, I had my arsenal ready. He'd suggested a book about a man who'd clinically died, but wasn't totally on the other side. The man struggled to give his wife and others clues that he wasn't dead. I tried to read this book, but about a third of the way through, I realized I needed more positive, less-morbid readings. Before Hal left, he wished me luck, gave me his number, and told me I'd be fine because I really was a great candidate. Hal was a great inspiration, and I felt much better about what I was facing after talking with him.

I began to settle in as the new guy, and eventually moved up in order as people either moved to different parts of the hospital, went home, received transplants, or even, in some unfortunate cases, died. This was my life, and as hard as it was, I tried to stay positive. It was a tall order for me—an even taller one for my wife. Nikki was oblivious to a lot of the information concerning my situation because I chose to tell her only "just enough."

The Bronx Girl

My life consisted of many sleepless nights filled with prayers for good health. I had learned a long time ago to pray for you first, and then pray for others. This prayer sequence allows you to receive your blessings first, and then you're able to reach out and lift up those around you. I had many people depending on me; I really didn't want to leave them.

Nikki needed me as much as I needed her. As I lay in one place, I thought about how much she had to do each day to hold our family together. I wasn't so sure I would want to trade places with her. Here I was laying around waiting for a heart transplant, thinking I had it the worst, but did I? She was running herself ragged and she didn't know if she was about to lose her soul mate.

Nikki and I had met a few years prior to the onset of my condition. I already had four children, and was on the dwindling end of a long-term relationship. At the time I was a party promoter, which is how we officially met. Never one to make the first move, and already in a relationship, like a cheetah, I sat back and watched my prey. The truth is that if I lived in the jungle, I would starve because I let my prey walk away many times. I was in awe. I'd been involved with beautiful women before, but she was stunningly different, and this confused me. Initially, she paid me no attention at all. You see, I have never had problems with women. Actually I did have a problem with women—and that was being able to stay true to one. At that point, I couldn't make a move. I was afraid of being rejected.

Years later she called me about tickets to a comedy event that I planned. As the promoter, I purposely put my phone number last on the flyer. Nikki says she randomly chose a number. To this day, we joke about that since I still don't believe her. My pride says meeting her was fate. I'm not ready to concede that it was completely random.

During the first years we dated, I was the physically robust guy with no restrictions. Only a few years later she had to hear my complaints such as: I can't breathe, my stomach or liver feels full, or I'm so tired. This had to be hard on her because Nikki is the type to take control, and make things better. Now she was in a situation where there was nothing she could do other than be supportive, and not add stress. She became an absolute expert at this. The worse I became, the more nurturing she became. As the doctors added sodium restrictions, she adapted her cooking. Going through airport metal detectors had been eventful because of the pacemaker, but she'd wait for me patiently on the other side. Even at tender, sensual moments, when my mind said yes but my body said no, she'd been very supportive. The debilitating part of my disease started to make me feel like less of a man. Shoveling snow, taking out the garbage, bringing in the groceries, Nikki didn't bat an eye. Things simply got done, and she never complained.

There was something about her, and I always knew it. She grew up tough as a Bronx girl. She was also the oldest out of three, and we shared a lot in common, especially our relationships with our mothers. She continuously proved to me she was in it for the long haul. I knew that she was the one. Still though, I worried about her. *How long could she keep this up? When would she need to take a break?* I had medicine for my problems, but I didn't have any medicine to help her understand that we would be all right.

Day in, day out, she would bring everything I needed or wanted to the hospital. She never called to say, "I'm tired," or "the weather is too bad." She always made it, no matter what, and I knew she knew if the tables ever turned, I would do the same thing.

My wife was a fixture at the hospital usually coming straight from work in her blue utility uniform. At one point, she snuck a Panini sandwich maker in my room, and treated the nurses to something different. Yes, she took care of everyone and everything. Her visits lasted from 5:15 p.m. after she worked all day, to 10p.m., traveling thirty minutes to the hospital.

On weekends she'd come about mid-morning and stay until dinner, unless she spent the night. If she stayed all night, it meant I got a great breakfast from the deli down the street the next morning—with real eggs. In the hospital, you would almost have to kill someone to get real eggs. Still I stuck to egg whites because I was always conscious of the 200+ milligrams of cholesterol per egg. Of course, I forgot this ideology when I gobbled up a rare serving of greasy sausage.

I prayed to get a successful heart transplant—if for no other reason than to repay this great woman. She took the workload off the nurses as she answered all of my little requests. And, of course, she was the only one giving me bed baths. I appreciated her for that. She'd watch my daily ritual of TV shows before nestling into her own chair next to my bed. The next morning she'd complain of all the noise from bells, whistles, buzzers, blood, and temperature takers. I would laugh and say, "Welcome to my world." Although I loved it, I really didn't want her to stay overnight in the hospital because: She needed her rest, and we had a teenage daughter at home. Getting her rest was one thing, but as all parents of teenagers know, leaving them along was an uneasy situation for the obvious reasons.

Our daughter, De'Asia, is a typical teenager. Technically she is my stepdaughter (I hate that word), but I've helped raise her since she was three, and I love her like my own flesh and blood. She's like one of those ice creams with the hard outer shell but soft on the inside. A very smart girl, she's always challenging you with question after question, and an insatiable desire to know why. I don't believe De'Asia will ever know how much she's taught me about women, specifically her mom. She made realize how moody women can get for no apparent reason and her indecisiveness had to be genetic.

The older she got, the more I let her know about my illness. Telling her I just couldn't walk too far was simply not going to cut it. She had to know why. As I would prepare her dinner, she would ask why my meal looked different than everyone else's. Of course, I'd have to explain the whole-low sodium, low-fat diet thing. The closer she got to her teens, the worse my condition grew. She needed more attention at this crucial segment of her life, but I had trouble even taking care of me.

Her actions reminded me how selfish kids could be. Most mean well though, and she taught me that teenage girls become even more selfish than boys. There's a whole "me-first" attitude, but I learned to accept it and roll with it. De'Asia, the girl with so much potential, would never know the stress she brought on her mom indirectly affected my health. As I got the phone calls or talks from her mom about teen girl stuff, my heart would race, putting me at the brink of an episode. So many times I wanted to ring her neck, but unlike my sons, scare tactics were useless. De'Asia was a great big-hearted teddy bear, but she succumbed to peer pressure more than the others.

We travelled near and far going to her basketball games, and even when I became so sick that I couldn't travel, I was very proud when she'd report back about a tournament. It pained me when I couldn't be there to support her because I knew how much she needed me. Daughters need their dads. In the latter part of my illness, prior to the hospitalization, I slept downstairs on the pullout bed with three pillows, and with my feet elevated. I often had massive coughing spells, and I could hear the concern in her voice as she'd try to help me. All in all she was scared—for herself, but I think more so for her mother. Every so often De'Asia would come with her mom to the hospital, but I knew she only wanted to see me for a short while, and then get the hell out of there. She was a teenager, for Christ sakes. I probably would have felt the same way. Keeping this in mind made it very important for my wife to be home whenever possible.

Sundays were special as Nikki and I would work on projects or pay bills while sitting on my bed. We'd reminisce about better times, and I'd remind her that one day I'd be home again taking care of them as usual. I'm not sure if she believed me, judging from the tears that ran down her cheeks. She'd have her moments, hell, *we'd* both have moments when our emotions overwhelmed us, but I sincerely felt it was not over for me. My life was not doomed. Nikki was on the front line with me, and didn't deserve this, I thought, so I had to get better. As I watched her leave some evenings, I imagined her path through the halls as she toted all of her bags. I looked out my window and waited to see her on the street. Light snow fell, as did my tears, as I watched this stalwart woman walk to her car. Before opening the door, she would glance up, knowing I'd be watching, and wave and wave. We never said "goodbye," as one of my cousins reminded me that goodbye is forever. But in my old piece of a heart, I believed I would see her again tomorrow. Nikki couldn't see my eyes nor could I see hers, but we believed. Softly I'd whisper, "Don't worry, dear; I'll still be here tomorrow." Then I hoped, and I prayed—even harder.

Support Groups

One particular Sunday, Nikki watched me as I gazed through the window, peering into the outside world that I longed to see again. I'm sure she was wondering what was I was thinking that day. Little did she know, my mind was flooded with horrible thoughts. I chose to keep these surreal images to myself because I didn't want to add to her burdens. Her plate was more than full.

We had taken an afternoon walk around the fifth floor, and ended up by the elevators. We watched nurses bring patients down who appeared to be heavily sedated. Later, I found out that those patients had been transplanted. If they weren't dead, they had to be as close as one could come. It was at that point I asked my wife to please put my tongue back in my mouth if I were lucky enough to receive a transplant. I didn't want to be seen like that. If something went wrong, I didn't want that vision to be the one ingrained in my loved ones' memories, especially my children's. This prompted me to question whether my feelings were mere vanity or an illustration of compassion instead. I chose the latter.

There was an even bigger question for me that day too. Looking out the window, I could see the George Washington Bridge, which I'd cross to go home. *Would I ever be able to travel across that bridge again alive?* Fearful emotions kicked in. I was having a breakdown, and Nikki could neither console nor help me this time. Physically I wasn't alone, but I slipped into mental isolation, which made me finally realize I needed to go to support groups.

I had always heard and read about support groups for various illnesses and problems, but I'd never taken a true interest. Why? Because I never thought I had a reason. Various people in my life might have been alcoholics and drug addicts, but I always thought those were their demons, and they'd eventually handle their issues for themselves. I thought it was simply mind over matter. I was wrong. Sick is sick, and sometimes it takes a lot more to help conquer a substance-abuse problem or worst yet, a mental issue. While in the hospital, I noticed that support groups for everything and everyone were everywhere. I actually saw a support group for people who suffer from going to too many support groups. Initially, I couldn't understand why people went back to groups over and over again, but that thinking would soon change.

Days after my semi-breakdown, and still not feeling my best, my social worker Elizabeth came in to talk to me about going to a support group. She explained that the people in the group were all waiting for a transplant or had already had theirs. For the first time in my life, a support group interested me. I decided to attend the group meeting with my wife that evening. I thought maybe I could gain some insight into my sudden moodiness. Walking into the meeting, I noticed some people were in hospital gowns and some in regular street clothes. I was in hospital pants, a tee shirt, and sneakers. I was still struggling with the allowing people to know how sick I was. Twenty minutes into the meeting, my feet began to become incredibly swollen from water retention so I slide them out of my sneakers. Luckily, no one noticed since I'd pulled up so close to the table. Later I discovered that none of this mattered to anyone in the group because most of us shared so much in common—we identified with one another. We were all over the map. There were patients in wheelchairs, who were too weak to walk, and some patients in great shape nearly twenty years post-transplant. Another thing I noticed was a clicking noise that was faintly audible. I discovered a few patients were on a Left Ventricular Assistance Device (LVAD). This little pump helped a pre-transplant patient's heart beat more efficiently, a sort of bridge between pre-transplant and transplant. Sometimes the patient would have to leave the room to go change his or her battery. For those in regular clothing, I wasn't really sure what their role was since they could not be easily identified. Were they doctors, social workers, or perhaps guest speakers?

After we all introduced ourselves, it became apparent that the street-clothed people were either waiting or had already received a transplant. I was astonished because I didn't know these "regular" folks were among us. I thought most of us who were in dire straits had some type of hospital garb to distinguish us from the healthy. If I were to have put my jeans on, I would have looked like them. I still had the ability to pass for normal. I was under the impression that most people would have been older or at least sickly looking. As crazy as it sounds, this turned out to be very comforting. There were people in the room who were just like me. Come to find out, I wasn't as "unlikely" as I first imagined. The funny thing about society is that no matter how much you say that you're not prejudiced, you can still have a prejudicial attitude.

I am an African-American who went to a predominantly white high school. Even though I met with some racism here and there, nothing turned me away from any one group of people. After high school, I went to a historically black college and although I had hundreds of non-black friends in high school, in college it felt natural to feel more comfortable in a predominately black setting. It's a concept most people find hard to admit, but it's real. I found that support groups made me react in a similar manner. Here in the heart transplant support group, I felt at home. Everyone was fighting against the same enemy: Death.

Sure, heart transplant people and "outsiders" share similar issues such as taxes, bills, unruly kids, choosing Starbucks or Dunkin Donuts, etc. but unless you're hit with a live-or-die situation, you'll never understand what that bond is like. Although taxes seem like a slow death, they fail in comparison to fainting from heart malfunction or a defibrillator firing. These sorts of life threatening traumas almost make tax time a welcome sight.

In group, after introductions, everyone shared why they came. I glanced about the room, impressed with how normal all the post-transplant patients looked, except for wearing their ever-present surgical masks. I'm not sure what I expected, but it certainly wasn't this. Their ages ranged from twenty-two to sixty-two.

I especially admired twenty-three-year-old Jason. He had so much energy and personality that you would never have imagined he was waiting on a heart to save his life. He inspired me because he was a young adult who should have been on his way to achieving his dreams. At some point, he, too, had become so sick and was hit with the grim news: The only real way to get his life close to normal would be a heart transplant. For me, at age forty-five, this had been incredibly shocking news, so at twenty-three, it had to be gut wrenching, His style and grace reminded me that sometimes GOD's plan is not always in black and white, or what we imagine it to be. Sometimes we have to be patient and let life play out. Jason had barely lived yet, and still his attitude was trumping my good approach to our situation.

Bob, who had been relegated to a wheelchair, was interesting. He had been sick for years, but over the last ten months, his health had declined sharply. He had been an athletic man and an avid weightlifter like me, but had now dropped almost eighty pounds in eight months due to his illness. Listening to him speak, he sounded as if he had lost his faith. He was on the transplant list, but something stood out about him that I will never forget. It seemed Bob was a man who had been pretty religious, or at least very faithful, at some point. He was able to recite all sorts of bible verses word for word. At one particular support group, the topic was actually faith versus religion. The majority of the group believed that our "fate" as patients was directly related to our "faith" in a higher power. Of course for me this was GOD. Bob thought much differently, however. He believed that our fate was circumstantial. He believed we would have to be more lucky than faithful to receive a heart. His theory was that, given a chance at a heart transplant, our fate was in the hands of our surgeon. To a degree, most of us agreed, but some like me thought it was GOD who helped guide the surgeon's hand, and would ultimately bring us through this major operation. Months later, Bob received his heart transplant, but due to complications, they were unable to close up his chest. Several weeks after his transplant, he died. It was believed the heart he received was too big for his body, and he eventually he died of infection.

As a person waiting on the list, this blew my mind. I wasn't sure how to make sense of the whole thing. Was it his lack of faith? Was it bad luck? Bob's death brought a sense of dread along with a great deal of sadness to the hospital. I prayed even harder to GOD, and I prayed for Bob's soul as well. At the support meetings, post-transplant patients brought a certain calming influence to the pre-transplant patients. People who had received their new hearts were naturally happier, and most were anxious to tell about their whole experience. I yearned to be like them since basically this was my persona anyway. As my wife and I sat in the meetings, people would share their stories, and a lot of them were pretty sad. Nikki, my super-sensitive Bronx-born wife could cry over road kill so she constantly clutched a box of tissues. We listened to each other as the "sick people" all gave their history, and shared how we looked forward to being better, even though we were very afraid of the unknown. As the stories flowed around the room, we all spoke about things that everybody could identify with. This was extremely rewarding since an outsider couldn't possibly understand what it was like to eat a slice of pizza, and hours later have your feet so swollen you couldn't wear your shoes from extra fluid build-up from salt retention. Men cried, because like me, their Congestive Heart Failure (CHF) wouldn't let them shovel snow or bring in bags of groceries anymore.

The post-transplant people rewarded us with their own stories, which always brought tears of joy. They explained that the surgery itself wasn't that bad, and that life would not only return as it was, but would be unbelievably better. For most of us, this was hard to imagine since the majority of people in the room had been battling illness for so long.

Dan, who had his surgery fifteen months earlier, particularly intrigued me. He was tall and looked very strong. We had similar body types (my old body at least). Looking at him, gave me so much hope, because I used to be him. This prompted me to ask Dan how long it took to get back to that size. He explained that he gained weight gradually over eight to ten months, I smiled internally, thinking, *I could do that*! Dan never knew, but he became my model heart-transplant guy. I found out that he used to work construction, but due to certain restrictions, like dust in the air, he couldn't do that work anymore. This was news I didn't want to accept for myself, but I realized our jobs and situations were obviously different.

One aspect that I hadn't considered was how vital the caretaker's role was. I watched Nikki, day in and day out, handle so many things most people could not begin to fathom, much less do. And she did it all without complaint. Like other transplant patients, I thought my job was the hardest, since I was the one waiting, getting cut, poked, biopsied, and of course having to eat hospital food. No. We found out that the caretaker's job was much more difficult. Not only did the caretaker have to be at our beck and call, but they also had to take care of the home and the children as well as go to most of the patient's appointments. They spent countless hours traveling back and forth to the hospital, spending the night in a small and uncomfortable chair beside a loved one's bed to save money on gas. Cutting grass, raking leaves, shoveling snow or carrying groceries all became the caretaker's job. For women caretakers, these tasks were heavy burdens—physically and emotionally.

Then there was the biggest hurdle of all—the caretaker had to deal with the possibility their loved one would not make it—and she or he would have to go on alone. We were reminded that many of them cried every night.

As a patient, we thought about death constantly, with one big difference. If we didn't pull through, we were done with the worries. But caretakers were left with all our baggage. They would be left to mourn, and to run a household on half of the physical, and, sometimes financial resources. The majority of the tears came from the caretakers because they dealt with different emotions and pressures, which I'm sure, were overwhelming, as well as dealing with all of our gripes. By far, their job was the most difficult.

In essence, the support groups helped me immensely. They probably helped Nikki even more since she was able to see and hear people who spoke from her vantage point. Many transplant patients came from very far away to share their stories and gather energy from all those in the room. I came to realize that these people would become my new fraternity. I had no clue how long I'd be waiting for a heart, but one thing was for sure: I'd be lapping up the support of those who were waiting with me, especially the fortunate people who made it to the "other side." Because of my social worker's encouragement to attend the support group, I had new hope that I would indeed make the trip back across the George Washington Bridge one day.

Family and Friends

Two weeks into my stay, I learned a new phrase: "Hurry up and wait." I had a few friends in prison who said, "do the time and don't let it do you." They'd tell me that's how they survived their long stretches of incarceration. I began to employ that philosophy because the everyday monotony of hospital life was grueling. Obviously not as grueling as prison, but grueling nonetheless. Prisoners often befriend correction officers, so they can live on the outside vicariously through them. That's exactly what I found myself doing with my nurses.

It became important for me to know about Nurse Katy's newborn son, what car her husband wanted to buy or Nurse Robinson's love life and how the party went on her day off. We shared many stories. And even though I couldn't leave the hospital physically, my mind was able to travel outside of the hospital's boundaries through their lives. These nurses became my two favorites, and I leaned on them. These caring women were great at their jobs, which included making me, their patient, feel special. I was happiest when they were assigned to me on any given day and I'm sure being such a low-maintenance patient, they enjoyed taking care of me.

The staff was important to all of us as patients because when all our visitors left, they were still there. Nikki worked all day in the freezing cold as a first class meter tester for the utility company, go home, cook something, and bring it to me by dinnertime. Then she would stay until I reluctantly forced her to go home. As usual, I hoped to catch a glimpse of her through the window. I was tired of being sick, weak, and alone. I was tired of this damn crying. I had to remind myself that I was a grown man, and I tried in vain to convince myself grown men don't get all emotional. It's a hard thing to wait on something to come when you're not sure when and if it will actually be coming. It was a little more stressful than say, waiting for a bus to come. At least you know your bus is coming, and if it by chance it doesn't, there's always a number to call. Of course, that's not the case waiting for a transplant. The likelihood of an organ becoming available depends on many other variables. Fortunately, I met yet another staff member who helped my wait go even smoother.

Mr. Lincoln was a blood technician who worked the three-to-eleven night shift. This was the time of day and evening when I had the least amount of activity, especially when I gave Nikki the night off or I suggested that she go home early to get some much-needed rest. Although it didn't happen often, she'd sometimes take me up on my offer. I met Mr. Lincoln in the lounge one evening, and we immediately hit it off. He was a tall black man about my age, with kids, and he loved sports. Of course, we started talking about the game on TV. Then our conversations would get extremely deep, and then I'd be summoned by a nurse to check my vital signs or to take my medicine and we would end up in my room. Some nights we'd talk for as long as five hours. His pager would go off sometimes, and he'd have to go to another part of the hospital, but he would come right back and we would continue where we left off. I always wondered how he got away with this, but I know he was no slouch at his job. His peers and repeat patients respected him. He introduced me to other heart transplant patients and key members of staff, and truly made me feel at home. He knew about my whole family, my life, and vice versa. I admired the fact that he was a vegan who really took care of his body, and although sports was one of our main topics of discussion, hospital gossip became another. This man knew about everything and everyone, and since all I had was time, I listened like a little kid being read a bedtime story. Lincoln was a good guy, and I looked forward to him coming on shift each day. He made me feel like a regular person who just happened to be sick for the moment. Lincoln would always say, "When you get out of this… When you leave this hospital…" I understood his attitude was coupled with the fact that he had already seen this scenario play out many times. But his demeanor and optimism reinforced my positivity. However, watching all the illness and death around me started to affect me, and I began to lean a bit to the negative side.

Each day was pretty much the same: breakfast, lunch and dinner, with a few snacks in between. Most times I didn't want to get up because of the difficulty sleeping at night, but housekeeping, or more specifically Tiondra, would serve as my alarm clock. She was another great staff member with whom I bonded, and loved listening to her tell stories about her family. Since I had no other major ailments, I was able to walk around, which gave Tiondra the ability to clean my room without me being in her way. I spoiled her a bit too much though. Some days I didn't really feel like getting up and out of my room, but because she was now my friend, I did. A lot of times she rewarded me at lunchtime with some great conversation. By now, my room became a hiding spot for Tiondra and the other staff members I befriended. I certainly welcomed this. Mentally, I needed the diversion and thought of my room as Smitty's man cave or a place to entertain. They probably had no clue that I was using them as much as they were using me, which made for a great mutual relationship.

Since I didn't know how long I'd be waiting for the transplant, so I needed ways to occupy my time. Visitors helped fill the dead zones. Naturally, my wife filled the bulk of the visit time, but many others also visited.

My sisters-in-law, Donna and Ty came by a couple of times. Truthfully, I didn't really expect too much from them because between them they had five children. I felt they had many other obligations, but Nikki saw it a little differently. She was stressed, emotional, and very hurt because no one offered to help her or help with De'Asia. We'd remind ourselves "people are different." Just because Nikki was the oldest in her family and knew what to say or when to jump in, and did it, didn't mean that others did too. I explained that I felt the same way about my brothers. But that was a losing battle because women are so different when it comes to their emotions. The absolute bottom line is that most people, including family, didn't know the magnitude of what we were going through. And, even if we'd told them, it might not have changed things. I still felt grateful for anyone who visited.

My younger brothers visited as well, and although Keith wasn't around much, he came when he could as did Bo. I'd always had the pleasure of looking out for both of them. They are my best friends. Keith the NFL Football Player and Bo the Bouncer—we've always been pretty close, sharing everything from clothes to cars. I'm sure it was painful for them to see their older brother in this helpless state.

Keith, who is the youngest and has a different father than Bo and me, was raised by all of us. He had everything, but yet nothing. He was always given great "hand-me downs" and even ended up living in an affluent neighborhood as a young teen when Bo and I were out of the house. But when my mom fell into a rough spot, a friend ended up caring Keith. He was the baby so he'd never had the misfortune of seeing roaches or living in squalor-like conditions like we did growing up. However, since he had no relationship with his father, I felt he always carried a chip on his shoulder.

A University of Syracuse ball player, Keith never truly knew the sacrifices I made trying to get up that hill or the stairs at the Carrier Dome. Never one to complain, I simply had to see my little brother play. Missing one of his college games was not an option. He knew I had a heart problem, but like everyone else, he had his own life, and furthermore, I always had my poker face on, so almost no one knew exactly how bad it was.

I couldn't let my brother down for a couple of reasons. First, I knew how important it was for him to have my support because as he often said, I was the closest thing he had to a real dad. The second was that I felt guilty because, at times, I'd let him down as a big brother. It was typical sibling stuff, nothing really serious, but when I was younger I had a lot of things going on in my life and I pushed my little brothers to the back burner. Keith never knew that my very first heart incident almost happened at one of his high school games. While standing on a hill in the middle of a game, I felt faint, and envisioned myself rolling down the hill. Fortunately, I caught myself in time—more likely, my heart went back into its normal rhythm. Today I realize I would have been embarrassed more for Keith than myself. I wanted to keep up a good reputation for my brother. I couldn't let it be known that Keith Bulluck had an ailing brother. At his college I had to go drink for drink, shot for shot. After he made it to the NFL, it was more of the same except now it was trips to Miami, California, Vegas, and Hawaii. Maintaining both my reputation and my brother's, he never guessed how close my body flirted with episodes, and how horrible I would feel for days afterwards.

Occasionally when Keith asked me how I felt, I would try to describe it in terms a non-cardiac patient could comprehend. I might say, "Man, it's like someone constantly squeezing my neck," referring to persistent pressure and shortness of breath. He'd take this in stride, saying, "Man you are going to be all right." This was role reversal—coming from the young man who looked to me as his father figure. Now he was coming to see me in a hospital, and even with all his fame and fortune, he couldn't do a thing to speed my healing.

Every now and then, brother Bo would surprise me with a visit. He was the perennial strong, tough brother, but I knew that since losing our father, he hated hospitals. Bo and I were six years apart, which made us a little closer, whereas Keith was fifteen years than me. I was in charge of Bo when we were young, so I learned his habits early, and sometimes he had mean tendencies. I never figured out where all that extra frustration came from, he probably still doesn't know either.

We ended up like Frick and Frack or Ying and Yang. I was the nice guy, analytical, and always thinking, the people person. Bo was somewhat unapproachable, cautious and extremely protective of his family. He was his own person, but I know he looked up to me a lot. I shared with him a lot about how I was feeling. The sicker I got, the more I could see his concern. Never one to say much, I could still read his expressions. Our father had died in front of us, and I learned a lot about my brother from that experience. Illness and death was truly not his thing, but he and I were too close for me not to honestly share the progression of my disease. This was not meant to scare him, but to educate him and persuade him to stay on top of his own health problems, like high-blood pressure and his bouts with gout. Having considered the possibility of my not being here, I'm positive the possibility was ripping him apart. His father, and now maybe his older brother might die? He certainly couldn't handle this. Maybe this is the reason he didn't make many doctor or hospital visits. Whatever the case, I certainly didn't fault him because I came to live by a simple statement: "people are different." I certainly wouldn't infringe on my brother's tough-guy personae, even when I might have wanted him to accompany me to the doctor. I'm sure my brother wanted my heart problems to simply go away, with a different result than our dad. I was happy to have him around the hospital, and cherished the time we spent alone together in manly conversation, because he had two kids, two jobs and a wife.

My sons KJ and Jared were much like Keith and Bo. KJ came when he could get time off from his second year with the Miami Dolphins. Jared would come when he wasn't in class or caring for their mom. Ironically, it was around this same time their mom, Felicia, began to get sick as well.

Instead of strictly concentrating on earning his keep as a new pro ball player, KJ had other issues, including visiting his ill father. It had to be a tall task when both your mom and dad were sick, He'd never known how extremely difficult it had been for me to attend his games and walk up high in the bleachers. He didn't know the number of times I almost fainted while jogging around taping live footage of his games. He didn't know how I had to suppress my elation when he made an outstanding play, so I wouldn't lose my breath. He was Kelvin Jr., so it was important for him to always see me as the strong, never-wavering head of the family. My son never knew I had to be dropped off at the front gate of the Carrier Dome because walking up the hill would almost kill me. He definitely didn't know that when we sat in the movies and he'd ask "Dad, you all right?" and I'd say, "yeah, why?" I was embarrassed by his reply, "Because you're breathing so heavily." I was sitting down, totally still, but never noticed. I was happy to be sitting there participating in our coveted father-and-son ritual of going to the movies. I'd been able to hide a lot of things, but not everything.

Of course, now I was fully exposed. No more hiding my sickness as I lay in bed, a frail man. Looking up at my son gave me a glimpse of what I used to be. The thought was chilling because I'm certain my father probably had the same thoughts as he lay dying in his hospital bed.

Jared, who is six years younger than KJ, is the smart guy with the ability to break down everything analytically. His visits to the hospital were not as frequent, but I understood the teenage-boy phenomenon, besides, it was his last year of high school and he was trying to have fun. I'm sure it didn't seem like life was too fair his senior year, with both his dad and his mom sick. That's a mammoth situation even for an adult. As he got older, and started to realize I wasn't feeling well, he would actually talk to me a little about it. Knowing Jared, he had already researched the conditions that beset me. He would tell me how medicines such as Coumadin and Lasix functioned, and he'd also explain the definition of mitral valve prolapse to me.

Because of my illness, I felt like I short-changed him on some things. Jared was a fair athlete who was a bit chunky during the height of my illness. I always wanted to jog and work out with him like I had with his brother. I'm from the school of "I can show you better than I can tell you." Physically I couldn't show him, so I felt that kept him from pushing himself. Sadly coaches said cruel things to him, partly because he was not his brother—a natural athlete, and partly because his weight affected his speed and agility. Hopefully, he knows now that might have been a blessing because he was forced to use his mind more than his body. GOD had a different plan for him. A very gifted writer and computer whiz, Jared has probably never realized I'm as proud of him as I am of his brother.

I only hope he now understands that those times when he wanted to go to the mall—and I'd tell him no because I wasn't feeling too well—I was afraid of the walk from the parking lot. I think he probably figured it out when I was able to play one-on-one basketball in the driveway for only two minutes. I was hoping the hospital surroundings would inspire Jared to lean towards the medical field. Perhaps this would be the silver lining we've been looking for. He's just so doggone smart.

I miss my father who had been there for me at the beginning stages of this terrible illness. It's strange how life works; I temporarily got better, and then he died. Within a year of becoming sick, he succumbed to colon cancer. It seemed as though I had truly become my dad, and now I was the one in a hospital bed having everyone come see me off, as we did him. I prayed for a different outcome. I believed I would see him again in a different world, but I hoped it would be later rather than sooner. My stepmother Senora comforted me the same way she had my father. I had to make through this to be there for her as well. I didn't want her to lose another of one of her men. She came all the way from North Carolina at different times, and stayed for weeks. This was the most assistance Nikki received, and we were grateful.

Sometimes I felt a little disappointed that my family didn't see me as much as I think I would have seen them, if roles were reversed. I'm the type to go the extra mile all of the time. It's my nature. I could not, nor did I want to, imagine one of my friends or family members knocking on death's door. My father's death taught me a valuable lesson that we should love hard and often, before it's too late. Without Nikki, I would have been lost, but everyone needs his or her whole family. My family probably thought I was in control, but sometimes I was not. My life was small—a hospital room—which gave me time to think and assess everything. I wasn't bitter, and didn't hold a grudge, but I knew if GOD afforded me a new chance at this thing called life, then I would take full advantage of every moment.

From old football coaches to celebrity friends, they all passed by at some point. My many visitors helped time speed up a bit. However, that big clock on my wall still read in hours, not days or weeks. After all my visitors had gone, I'd peek out my window hoping to catch a glimpse of them. Eventually, I'd say my prayers and slide into bed. Alone with that annoying clock, I continued to hurry up and wait.

Hurry Up and Wait

If heart disease didn't kill me, the anticipation was definitely taking its toll. Lying around the hospital for two plus months was giving me cabin fever. My mind was starting to be affected, occasionally turning me into a grumpy person, which was certainly not my nature. I tried my best to stay on an even keel, exercising my mind by writing. Although I knew I couldn't "jump" the transplant line, I still tried to be the best patient ever. I took a certain pride in everyone saying, "I don't know how you do it." I think it was my obsession with wanting to always be the best. To pass the time I also read, anything and everything I could get my hands on. When I didn't have visitors, I watched TV and my growing DVD collection.

TV and movies took my mind away from the obvious fact that I was extremely sick. I faked it so well in front of everyone, but I learned not to fake my doctors out, because as crazy as it sounds, I *wanted* to be in the hospital. I felt more secure here with medical help a call away. I didn't want to stay forever, but it was starting to feel as though that might be the case. The underlying truth was: I was afraid of dying. Not death, I was scared of the act of dying. Death was final, but dying was death on its way. It's like an airplane crash. The airplane's going straight down, you're dying. The airplane hits the ground. Boom! You're dead. It's simplistic, but true.

Out of the hospital, I had no safety net, but inside I felt I had a fighting chance to conquer death. I decided to tell all the decision makers how I really felt—from the simplest ailment to the most severe. When doctors would ask for permission, I even shared my sick body with med students, having many exams orchestrated by these future lifesavers. I had become the ultimate guinea pig. Essentially I wanted to help because these students might possibly be the ones who were able help others like me down the line. One by one, they'd poke and prod, telling me I looked so great they couldn't believe I was on the transplant list. Then I would jump into my spiel about my trials and tribulations—how I really felt physically. We'd laugh as I told them to never judge a book by its cover because, inside the pages could be falling apart. I was in the hospital so long that some med students were now teaching the new students about my medical history. I always stopped watching TV to say that I'd be happy to let all of them examine me. The exams were fully voluntary. I saw it as a way of giving back.

Preparing for a heart transplant was a lot like going to the NFL draft. The difference was that at this combine; (where players are poked, prodded and evaluated) no general managers would be watching your workout as they prepared to give you millions of dollars. Instead, top medical personnel would evaluate how you did on all of your tests. This determined where you would rank on the transplant list. So many people had to be seen in order to get you ready for transplant.

One particular specialist was a physical therapist. In essence, the P.T. was my trainer. All I really wanted to do was lie around and wait until transplant day. Quickly, I learned this was not going to happen. The therapist, and most hospital personnel, wanted me to constantly work. At the time, I couldn't understand this because I felt so bad physically, why would they want me to push my existing heart to the brink of destruction? Since I felt like it could give out at any second, doing physical therapy was incomprehensible to me. The therapist would have me do certain exercises that would elevate my heart rate, like quickly walking up and down the stairs. After my defibrillator episode in the gym, I was deathly afraid to do anything strenuous. The mere thought of having it fire made me want to faint. The therapist had me totally hooked up to monitors, and didn't allow me to overdo. Once she saw my heart's rhythm getting wacky, she'd have me stop immediately, and then note how long it took for my heart to return to normal. She also had me do strength exercises, but these didn't scare me because they weren't as heavy a draw on my heart. She was always positive and made me feel as though I was passing all the tests. Passing the tests was actually failing the test for normal people, but my entire class was in line for a heart transplant patient—and she graded on a curve. It wasn't her job to determine if I was eligible, that had been determined already. It was her job to make sure I was still as sick as my records indicated, and that my diseased heart hadn't suddenly made a miraculous turnaround. It obviously had not.

I had so many procedures done on me. Some were weird, such as neurology testing to make sure my nervous system wasn't damaged. This test actually tickled as the electrodes that were attached made different muscles twitch. Painful procedures, such as the muscle biopsy taken underneath my left bicep, determined if there was any damage to muscle tissue. This hurt pretty badly as it required the doctor to make an incision and lift the fibers of muscle to get a good slice of tissue for the lab to sample.

But, by far, the most painful procedure of them all was the bone tissue biopsy. The sample was taken through my lower back into my pelvic bone. I could tell I was in for a ride by the way the doctor approached me, saying: "This isn't the most pleasant procedure." When a doctor says that, the direct translation is "there will be a world of pain on the way! No one had informed me about this test, and I'd never seen this particular doctor. He came to my room at 7 a.m., giving me a choice to do it later or right then. He was an oncologist who told me that some of my blood work showed an increase in cancer markers. He said it was probably nothing, but they needed to be more conclusive prior to transplant. I chose to do the test then, while I was still half sleep and didn't have time to think about it. I was told to lie on my stomach, and my lower back would be numbed prior to a gigantic needle drilling into my pelvic bone to pull out a core sample. Although my back was numb, I felt the blood running down my butt and starting to form a puddle under my stomach. I heard the needle piercing my pelvic bone. The crunching sound was nauseating, and the pain excruciating, causing a tear to run involuntarily down my cheek. I imagined an oilrig drilling through the earth's crust and core. I now understand why the doctor came to me so early in the morning, and why other doctors later told me how barbaric the procedure was. Finally there was a clear-cut winner as to what caused my body the most pain. Having had a bad root canal, now I would gladly have taken three on the same day rather than this torture. After thirty minutes, it was finally over, and as I lay there on my stomach, I felt violated, penetrated with a needle the size of the ones vets use on horses. I was so mentally and physically exhausted that after he left, I stared aimlessly out of my window for hours.

When I wasn't busy with procedures or visitors, I zoned into my little TV. I began to be a fan of shows I normally wouldn't watch. I tuned into all the judge shows: Alex, Christina, Judy, and Joe Brown. A lot of times they weren't even interesting, but I knew by watching, that my stay was one hour less. Sporting events were obviously my favorite pastime, and I tuned in to many basketball games in the beginning of my stay in the winter. When spring came, I felt less bored because the Yankees were playing. They were my favorite team, besides, a baseball game is typically three hours long, and it held my attention for its entirety. Baseball games reminded me that my time in the hospital was truly accumulating, considering that I was admitted two days after the Super Bowl. I made friends with the evening housekeeper who was an extreme Mets fan. Even though she had quite broken English, we were able to spar about the Yankees versus the Mets each time they played.

My DVD collection at home was excellent, but, of course, now in the hospital it had to be even better. When you're hospitalized, people always ask you if there is anything they can bring you. Most of the time I'd answer no, but select family and friends knew I'd love a new movie or interesting DVD to watch.

My brother Keith hit it out of the park with his choices, but I'd have to coach the others. TV series like The Sopranos, The Wire, The Office, I'd watch the entire set in a day and a half. The show Nip/Tuck I turned down for obvious reasons. My friend Rock thought I'd be interested in the movie "Awake," in which a cardiac patient's anesthesia never kicks in, leaving him awake and feeling everything during surgery. I assume Rock was trying to be funny. Seriously though, I needed action. I was in a hospital room for months, outside of terrifying procedures; I had no action at all. For the same reasons, I needed comedy. Obviously things weren't funny while waiting for such a serious surgery.

My personality still made me laugh through tears. So did the Martin TV comedy series. Actually, bringing me anything funny to watch was a safe bet. I'm sure I fooled some folks as I laughed hysterically, like my life wasn't hanging in the balance. Fortunately for me, GOD granted me the ability to be a little different. A lot of people stressed over the unforeseen future, but I had the uncanny gift of not stressing over things I couldn't control. I was adept at "rolling with the punches," and letting things happen as they may.

As the days rolled into weeks, and weeks into months, it certainly became tougher not to stress, but somehow I did my best, including staying focused. A long list of likely and unlikely visitors, writing in my diary, and being the best patient possible certainly helped. The mini hospital-issued flat-screen TV became the ultimate lifeline because when everyone was gone, it was my TV and me for unending hours. Mentally I might begin to waiver, but my TV was the last thing I saw at night and the first thing I saw in the morning—and I loved it like a best friend.

Sex, Drugs and Alcohol

11

Many television programs and movies center on hospital life. I have a better appreciation for them after being cast as a main character in my own. I witnessed the daily drama that made it the perfect arena from which producers could draw. My life became a movie within a movie. The hospital staff had their own thing going on, in addition to the patients. I could always count on Mr. Lincoln to give me the update on all the juicy hospital gossip. One particular night after he left, I lay in bed thinking about all of my "stuff." I thought about what Dr. Maxwell told me. He removed any doubts I had about me possibly bringing heart disease upon myself. "It was, in all probability, a genetic disorder," he said. I wanted to believe him. I *had* to believe him, otherwise the guilt would be crippling. Dr. Maxwell was a licensed professional—he had to be right. I was driving myself crazy wondering. I had done things like other folks, but not everyone lay waiting for a heart transplant. As Nurse Nyanne took my vitals, a painful memory caused me to re-evaluate my worthiness.

I know they say money makes the world go around, but living life each day, it's obvious reading tabloids, listening to, and watching the media, that sex obviously isn't far behind money. Sex had become important to me from an extremely young age. I did many things I'm not proud of, many things I had no control over, although in some instances I could have used better judgment.

Thus began my battle with promiscuity. The very first incident was with a girl named Cynthia, who was about my age. I remember quite vividly (like who wouldn't) behind her garage. The whole act took about three minutes, but from there I was off to the proverbial races. One event I had no control over was lying in the bed soon after with my fifteen year old babysitter and her little brothers and sister. I was strategically placed directly behind her. In the middle of the night, while I was innocently sleeping, I felt her reach behind her back and fondle me. Initially, the little boy in me thought it was all a dream. Then I realized what she was doing, she was pulling me into her. Sure I could have screamed and got up and ran out, but the truth was I think I liked it. I didn't know any better. Hell, I was seven or eight years old! I'm assuming she liked babysitting me because this happened a few times. Her maneuvers made me want more, yes, I liked my babysitter.

Not until my late thirties did I realize that I had actually been molested starting at age seven or eight by that babysitter. Unfortunately, Nurse Nyanne resembled that girl, and seeing her stirred up some old memories. I had dealt with everyone else's addictions and problems, now finally I was able to come up with this realization on my own. This girl changed my life.

Sex became a driving force, and was an extremely important part of my life. My relationships suffered greatly because one or two girls/women were simply not enough. The guys thought I was cool, and girls hated to love me. As I got older, I realized I was a jerk. I knew I'd been out of control for many years. Now I had a daunting task ahead of me; to convey the message to my sons that it wasn't cool at all to be a "player." It might have been age or maturity that made a light bulb go off or maybe the fact that I ended up having a daughter. It sounds like an excuse, but I'd had no male role model since most of my life I was raised by women. My grandmother, mother and aunt were great, but they could never know what it was like to think like a young man. This is why it's vitally important to have a father or strong male influence in a boy's life. That will always be something my dad and I missed due to our separation. Mom had moved us up to New York when I was seven after they split up.

As men, a lot of time we're measured, sometimes literally, by our sexual prowess. Like many men, I used mine to my so-called benefit. I always say GOD has a great sense of humor because when I thought I had "grown up," and didn't feel the need to use sex as a tool, things happened. Ironically, it was about the same time I began having the heart problems that I noticed that things were starting to affect me sexually, which some might say was bad karma. Most men will understand a little better than women when I say, "my soldier" didn't stand up as tall anymore. I began to experience erectile dysfunction (ED). Me, I thought? This was totally unacceptable! I didn't want to talk to anyone about it, and like many men, I used every excuse in the book like, "I'm so exhausted today," or "I have a lot on my mind," or "the damn Yankees lost!" _

I had heard about men having these types of issues, but I sort of scoffed at it ever happening to me. To be honest, the timing couldn't have been better. This probably sounds incredibly confusing. It's not like I embraced ED, but the fact that it was happening at the end of my promiscuous days was a plus. When I met Nikki, and was with her, I never had to be the big macho guy. She convinced me she was in this battle with me, so she completely understood that my heart condition was starting to inhibit my circulation.

My pride wouldn't allow me to try prescription drugs to combat the ED problem. Heart failure was now affecting my sex life and this was important. As understanding as Nikki was, I'm sure it was just as important to her, but she never complained. Different heart medicines had various side effects, which enhanced the ED. I began to have pressure building in my liver, causing it to swell, and this swelling pushed against my lungs, which caused my shortness of breath. My heart was working overtime. Even though I felt like crap, and couldn't breathe, heart failure was challenging my manhood—many times winning. Sometimes during an intimate encounter, Nikki would ask if I was all right, and even though I'd reply yes, I really wasn't. Many times over the years I'd literally gasp for air as it felt as if my heart was going to beat out of my chest. These deficiencies were new to me. I felt like I had to please, Nikki hadn't signed up for this, and no way was I going to lose her because of it. Since my youth, sex had been my strong point. Another of my favorite sayings was, "Pride will kill you." Looking back of course, I realize she was not a shallow woman. In fact, she provided clarity to my inane thoughts on many occasions.

My doctor also asked me whether I took street drugs. This was not a job application where lying could help enhance your opportunity for hire—this was my life we were talking about. I felt the need to come clean because we're in a drug-driven era. Actually more specifically a marijuana-crazed era, and many people I know smoke it. I really don't understand what the obsession is, but I believe in being honest when dealing with the kids today. It was a drug I really didn't care for that much. The first time I tried weed I was in sixth grade. (Today I look around at all the people who think they're great parents, and realize they don't have a clue how young children experiment.) I smoked for three straight years.

I didn't really like its effect, because it made my fingers stink and stained my thumb and index finger. Marijuana always made me time-conscious. I bugged the hell out of my friends by constantly asking, "What time is it?" I did have a curfew, and I was never one to get in trouble. Although I wasn't a gullible kid, I might try something once, or maybe even twice. Weed shortened my breath, and also caused paranoia. Many times I'd go home high, carrying Visine for the redness in my eyes. For some reason, my mom never questioned me. I experimented once more in ninth grade, but realized weed wasn't my thing. I never tried it again until I was a college freshman. Mainly I stopped because I didn't really get off on the laid-back euphoria that came along with it. To me, it was a waste.

I find it downright hilarious when kids today, including my own, attempt to hide their "state of highness," as if we were born yesterday. Throughout my adult years, I smoked very sporadically. Also, in college, as was pretty typical, I tried everything that was available. I witnessed one of my roommates opening up a couple of capsules and dropping it in his beer. He told me it was speed. Never one to be a follower, I was intrigued because I thought this is what college students did. You let your hair down and experience new things. (I never said I was the smartest kid in the class). "Speed" really had no real effect on me, and I never tried it again.

However, one particular drug did have an effect on me. It was a Friday evening, and my roommate and I were out of class, chilling in our room. Away from home, it sometimes got a little boring at school. As I looked over at G, he proceeded to prepare a white powdery substance, eventually inhaling it through his nose. I was extremely hesitant about this one, because it didn't seem like something I wanted to try.

"Through your nose?" I attempted to reason. I asked him how it made him feel, and he said it made him feel like he was invincible, could do anything—like he was on top of the world. After that description, I had to try it. Sure enough, he was right. Only one thing: he'd forgotten to tell me—the drawbacks of cocaine. The fact that it numbed you, made you lose your appetite, kept you awake, dilated your pupils, affected your speech, and most importantly, made your heart race were probably not a good thing.

Every other weekend or so throughout college I'd have some. I agreed when someone said that it's really only the first twenty minutes of euphoria the body craves. After that, your body is forever chasing the initial twenty minutes. After graduating from college, I went back home and introduced this "new" drug to my friends. We were all former or current athletes who'd taken a vow to never do dumb things such as hard drugs. However, as the oldest, I somehow convinced them it really wasn't that bad, and in fact it was quite good. Being the "great friend" that I was, I never mentioned the side effects either. We were respected in our community, and did it only on weekends, behind closed door—most of us, anyway. Some continued, progressing to harder drugs, and some, to this day, are still looking for that elusive first twenty minutes. Some mornings, I lay in bed watching the sunrise, praying my heart would slow down. Thinking back about how dumb that was makes me want to throw up. It took partying with a friend one early morning that made me stop doing drugs. As we rode around inebriated in my Jeep, I looked over at my friend as he bopped, sang and danced to the music. Only one problem: he was deaf. I never did drugs again.

I used alcohol at the same time I experimented with marijuana in sixth grade. It started with something called Mad Dog 20/20 or MD 20/20. It was a sweet drink, and its effect was a sneaky one. I found I didn't really like hard liquor very much, but did enjoy cold beer. It was an acquired tasted, and I acquired the taste much too often in college. Of course, during my college days I explored the hard stuff like Everclear grain alcohol, with skulls right on the bottle. Although the label clearly states that over-consumption could result in death. I still gave this a shot. From the massive hangovers I got, I learned quickly I didn't like getting drunk, but I did appreciate a cold beer and a buzz. As I got older, flying all over the nation to Super Bowls and many other massive events, I pushed my body to limits previously untested.

Once in Las Vegas with my brothers and friends, we stayed at a big expensive hotel. I had already been diagnosed with heart failure and was on a daily cocktail of medications, including blood thinners. One of my eyes was filled with blood from a broken capillary or two. I felt and looked horrible. My brothers and friends begged me to come down from the room and have dinner and drinks. No way should I have been there at all, but I couldn't let them see me be weak. I forced myself to drink hard liquor and hit the clubs with them. They had no clue that I was pushing my heart to the max. My pacemaker demanded I find a comfortable spot away from the loud speakers, so that its effectiveness wouldn't be compromised. I watched my brothers have fun, never knowing I couldn't wait for it to be over. I was simply there to appease them.

So now laying in this hospital bed for months with plenty of time to look back over my life, I knew I'd pushed my body to unknown limits with loads of sex, drugs, and alcohol. It was through the shear grace of GOD, I lived long enough to be considered for a second chance at life. I battled many demons, and made many bad decisions, but along the way I received many blessings. It was truly meaningful when my doctor told me my heart disease wasn't from abusing drugs or alcohol, although I'm sure it didn't help my already-diseased heart.

As Nurse Nyanne turned off my room lights, I thought about how abuse comes in all shapes and sizes—mine starting with the babysitter. I believe the sicker my heart got, the healthier my mind became, giving me the chance to learn a lot about who I was, and what I had become. As they say, "Whatever doesn't kill you makes you stronger." I found myself turning into Hercules. I prayed I would be able to stay alive long enough to prove myself worthy of a second chance.

The Call

12

Sometimes it seemed like the giant clock on the wall was going in reverse. Time seemed to drag. If I sound selfish, I am sorry, but I was tired of being the "sick one." I wanted something to happen. Now! I prayed for the best scenario because I knew I was in a special group of people throughout the world. There were thousands of people much worse off than me who were waiting for the bittersweet miracle.

On April 16, 2008 at 5:50 p.m., I heard a knock at my door. A nurse said, "Your doctor has been trying to reach you on your room phone." I had been on the phone with a co-worker who was telling me about a roofing job. As I excused myself from my co-worker, I told the nurse to let the doctor know she could call back anytime. My doctor this week was Dr. Fanning, who was filling in for Dr. Maxwell. Extremely nice, she was a stunning woman who looked like she could be related to Nicole Kidman. *Why was she was calling?* Only forty-five minutes ago, she had left my room after doing her nightly checks before leaving for the evening. My thoughts were suddenly interrupted as the phone rang. The conversation went something like this:

Dr. Fanning: "Hello Kelvin?"

Me:" Yes?"

Dr. Fanning: "I believe we have a heart for you."

Me: "You're kidding me, right?"

Dr. Fanning: "Not at all, I knew when I came to your room earlier, but I had to be sure it was a go."

Me: (silence)

Dr. Fanning: "You okay?"

Me: "Absolutely."

Dr. Fanning: "Alright, well it's time to start making some calls."

Me: "I sure will!"

Dr. Fanning: "You excited?"

Me: "Yes, but a little shocked."

Dr. Fanning: "Okay, well get going, and we'll get everything ready. Congratulations!"

Me: "Thank you so much."

Dr. Fanning: "No problem. You're welcome, and you deserve this."

Hanging up the phone, I sat on the edge of my bed thinking:

"What just happened?" Talk about surreal. This certainly felt like a dream. My mind, as well as my decrepit heart, was racing. Out of the million times the nurses ran to my room because my telemetry box showed rapid-heart movement, this time no one came. This was weird because I was sure my heart rhythm was way out of control. I tried to make myself relax because I certainly didn't want to *die NOW*. After almost three months, this was not the time to check out. In a short time I was to get a new life. I regained my composure. Next, I did the unimaginable; I called my co-worker back to let him finish his conversation. Even in a tense situation like this, I stayed true to my personality. I never thought about sharing my great news. Nikki deserved to be first to know she was a step closer to getting her husband back. Subconsciously, I think I returned my co-worker's call in order calm myself. Sometimes I amazed myself because I never tipped my hand about my good news. Now it was time for a much more important conversation. For what seemed to be an eternity, we had waited, and now the time had finally come. Breaking the news to Nikki without becoming emotional was going to be tough. When I reached her on the phone, she was in the hair salon. My job became a little more daunting since she now had an audience. I wanted her to try to keep her excitement to herself. As she answered, the conversation went like this:

> Me: "Hey, what you doing?"
>
> Nikki: "Nothing, I was at the beauty salon under the dryer. Is everything okay?"
>
> Me: "Yeah, nothing crazy."
>
> Nikki: "Okay, well I'm almost done, and then I'm on my way."
>
> Me: "Alright, please don't make any more stops along the way, okay?"
>
> Nikki: "I won't, but why?"

Me: "If I tell you something, do you promise to be cool?"

Nikki: "Yes!"

Me: "I got the call."

Nikki: "What call?"

Me: "They found a heart."

Nikki: "Oh my GOD! Oh my GOD! I'm on my way!"

Me: (through tears) "I said to be cool!"

Nikki: "OK! OK! (Whispering, Oh my GOD)."

Me: "Get yourself together, call Senora (my stepmom)."

Nikki: "When is it happening?"

Me: "About midnight. See you soon."

Nikki: "Okay, bye."

Simultaneously, we both hung up.

For two and half months I had held it together. I had waited so long for "the call," when I heard Nikki's voice I became emotional. It was such a foggy quest, but finally we could see a glimmer of light. Actually, it was more like a beacon of light. I could only imagine the anxiety she was having while sitting in the salon and not being able to tell. I knew this because I was having issues with my own anxiety. I walked into the bathroom and stared at the mirror. As tears streamed down my face into the sink, I prayed. I thanked GOD so much. He had brought yet another miracle to me, and I was extremely grateful. I knew I still had miles to go on my journey, but I couldn't travel without this vehicle. GOD summoned a jet that was literally on its way. I opened my gown and examined my skinny, semi-scarred chest, and imagined this would be the last day to see it looking like this. I was okay with it; within my old heart I felt I would soon be better. Yes, possibly one day soon I would be able to perform simple tasks that were out of my reach for the past ten years. I envisioned getting my manhood back like shoveling snow, raking leaves, having the ability to bring in more than one bag of groceries. I would welcome the return of all of it. The long tunnel had been so dark, but the call assured me that there was a light at the end. It was now time to get an entirely different game face on in preparation for the upcoming major event.

Suddenly like a ton of bricks, it hit me...*Someone had died!* Someone had to die in order for me to live. This was now a reality, and it, kind of, sucked. My emotions were all over the place. Who was it? How did they die? Did he or she have children? Was he or she a good individual? Was I, in fact, deserving of this miracle? Again, I had to trust in GOD. Only He knew the answers to my questions, and I knew He made no mistakes. Everything was all in His plan. I calmed down and left it to Him.

I had been told that once the call came, things would move kind of slow at first, but then speed up, appearing almost out of control. Different hospital personnel came to see me for various reasons—doctors, anesthesiologists, others—everyone came. There were papers to sign, which was expected. I signed documents that wouldn't hold the hospital liable in case something went incredibly awry. I'd always known there was a remote possibility, so I signed without giving it much thought. It was explained how my evening would go, and approximately what time they'd come for me. I learned it wouldn't be until about midnight, but after waiting over two plus months, a little longer wait was no big deal. The nurse on duty congratulated me, and told me not to tell anyone because it could be a false alarm. I agreed, but found this to be a little humorous because almost every nurse on the floor came to wish me well. The cat was already out the bag, which was fine because the well-wishers had been with me all along. Their shift was ending at seven, and they wanted to wish Mr. Smith good luck. This was an incredibly big deal to the staff; they took great pride in caring for me, as well as prepping me for my all-important day. One thing that was quite noticeable was my clock. Prior to "The Call," it was more of a sundial, but now with all of the hustle and bustle of getting me ready, it seemed like it actually began to speed up.

13

Game Time

The day had finally arrived, and a major buzz took over the hospital floor. I was the hot ticket. I'm sure there was excitement when the other heart patients had received their call, but because it didn't affect me directly, I'd been somewhat oblivious. It was my time now, and the self-centeredness of human flesh made me feel that all eyes were on me. I embraced the experience as if I was still playing in a big-time ball game. Like back then, it was time to focus, get fully prepared, and clear my mind as much as possible. The difference was that I had never been in a game like this before. In fact, this wasn't a game. This was life or death. I was as ready as I'd ever be.

Nikki arrived about 8:30, and we hugged, but really didn't talk about "The Call" at first. She was never one to be able to mask her emotions, so I asked her how she felt. Surprisingly she told me she was fine; a little excited, but fine. Her attitude comforted me because it meant I didn't have to worry about her, and could concentrate on getting ready.

She'd obviously paid attention in the support group meetings when we discussed what to do when you receive "The Call." She began to pack up all of my things, which after two and half months, had begun to accumulate. All of the packing actually triggered thoughts making me realize that this was it. I wouldn't be coming back to this room, which had become home. She worked feverishly getting everything ready for my departure by taking down pictures, cards, good-luck charms, sacred olive oil, and other faith-related items I prayed with every night. One other important item I noticed she put with my personal things was my Make-a-Wish trinket. This was a small metal box she'd purchased from one of her co-workers who sold it for their church. I made my wish, and folded the paper inside. I never shared with anyone what I'd wished for, and vowed never to remove the paper until I left the hospital.

Eventually, my brother Bo and my friend Ruben arrived. They came down on such short notice, which made up for all the lonely times I'd wished they had been there. They were here now. In a matter of hours, I'd either be really alive or really dead. Nikki had called them, and I was extremely grateful to have my brother and friend by my side. We shared some great jokes, as usual, which I found to be a bit strange. When my father was in the hospital fighting colon cancer, he joked with us the same exact way—but three days later he passed away. I'm not sure if Bo realized that, but I did. My father and I shared the same personality, so I knew if I was going out, I was going out my way. Dad did it, and so would I. I wanted to be remembered as someone who had laughed until the very end. We all joked about how they could see my rib cage through my tight, small gown. They even caught the remains of my shrunken little butt as I tried in vain to conceal it on the way to the bathroom. We all found it funny when I told them I hadn't eaten since 1 p.m., and even though I brushed my teeth, I felt my breath wasn't fresh. I asked them for gum, but it only made my stomach churn and become gassy. We were all laughing. This was the Smitty I hoped they would remember. I was determined to leave a lasting impression.

The laughter was soon put on hold as the two nurses came in around 11 p.m. to prep me for surgery. A veteran female nurse and a young male nurse were both knowledgeable about their jobs, but it was the male nurse who took the lead, even though he had never before prepped a transplant patient. His name was Johnson, and I wasn't really sure of his sexual orientation, mostly because he made me wonder when he spoke of my "nice muscle tone." "Are you kidding me?" I thought. I'd known veteran nurse Vicky since I first got to the hospital. She found Johnson's comments to be hilarious, and she doubled over with "side-splitting laughter" when it came time to shave my chest and groin area. The funny thing: I didn't really mind at all. It was too late to be sensitive. As midnight rolled around, we were all tired, but on high alert. Bo and Ruben hung in there, I couldn't convince them to go home. Nikki, who's been known to take a quick nap, wouldn't allow herself one that night. I was tired for different reasons, and every time someone walked near my door, I thought it was time to go. I had heard about false alarms before, and about 12:45 a.m., I was starting to think this was one. I knew from reading, support groups, and my doctors, that the whole heart transplant operation was about timing. It was after midnight so I thought I had possibly missed my time. Would I have to go back on the list? I was beginning to think it wasn't going to happen. Finally, about 12:55 a.m., they were at my door to take me to the operating room. As they got me onto the gurney, I knew it was official by the way they were dressed. They had scrubs with the hats and everything, like on a TV show. My anxiety grew. It was becoming harder to relax, but I tried. As I was wheeled past the nurses' station, everyone said their good-byes to Mr. Smith. It was at that moment I promised that when I made it through this, I'd come back and visit these very special people.

As the six of us began our journey to the O.R., I couldn't help but think this man on the gurney was a far cry from the man everyone came to for so many reasons. I was the self-proclaimed leader of my family, about to embark on a mission that most people have only heard about, read about, or seen on TV. We stopped at a room down the hall from the operating room, the green room—before the real deal. Another nurse came in as the other two momentarily left. There were more questions as well as more paperwork to sign. A curtain partitioned off the room, and the temperature was very cool. This coolness made me aware that I was close to the O.R. and its extremely sterile atmosphere. I asked for a blanket and another pillow to put under my back because by now I'd been on the gurney for three hours, and was starting to be very uncomfortable. The anesthesiologist came in and explained some pertinent things about the surgery, and also gave me some medicine to relax. I sensed my time was getting even closer, and I took this opportunity to ask Bo and Ruben to leave Nikki and me alone for the remainder of my wait. Ruben gave me his regards and a firm handshake. My brother, tough until the end, showed no sign of fear. He kissed me on the forehead, told me he loved me, and would be there when I woke up. I loved these guys for coming and waiting with me, especially because Bo was my little brother, and I knew he was very worried. I was supposed to always be here to protect him. I showed him no fear because the truth was, I wasn't afraid.

The last thirty minutes my wife and I were alone. Nikki was probably the strongest woman I'd ever known. Like me, she had a mother who went through some hardships, and she was also the eldest of three siblings. She was also her family's "go-to" person. She had once explained to me that I became her calming influence, and she now felt her life was complete. As I recalled that statement, I felt sorry for her. I felt sorry because she'd had a rough life, and now finally she had someone—but now there was a possibility this person might not be there. It's something I'm sure crossed her mind at some point because human nature allows us to be doubtful at times. However, she, too, showed no fear. Nikki stroked my arm and asked me if I was ready? I replied, "Ready as I'll ever be." I meant it. How much more ready can one get for a heart transplant? I'd been sick, as far I knew it, for at least ten years. I lay in a hospital bed for approximately seventy-five days. No more pre-game warm-ups. It was game time, and I was ready. I was forty-five, and had lived an incredible life, but I had so much more living to do. There were so many more things I wanted and needed to do with Nikki. I wanted to give her back the strong individual she fell in love with and married. In these last thirty minutes, we didn't discuss the surgery. We talked in general, mostly about the kids. I was ready to give her back her life as well. The forty-minute hurried trip back-and-forth to the hospital, after working all day, would now be over. One way or another, her life would soon change. Our conversation came to an abrupt halt as the two original nurses returned to bring me to the O.R. They, of course, asked me if I was ready. Yes! Again, the feelings were surreal as I was being wheeled away down the corridor. I kissed Nikki and joked, "I'll be right back." I watched the lights above me going by as we wheeled past, in what seemed like slow motion. Although I was praying on my way, I caught myself quoting bible scriptures that I'd never really known before like, "and though I walk through the valley of doom, I will fear no evil for thou art with me…" I looked back to my wife and threw up the peace sign as we entered the O.R. doors.

Inside the O.R., it was really chilly and extremely bright. It seemed each of the three medical people in the room specialized in certain areas. The anesthesiologist was busy preparing my right wrist for an I.V., and each of the other two was busy **sterilizing** my body. There was no sign of the surgeon—the star player—who I was sure wouldn't show up until I was totally ready for surgery, completely sterile and unconscious. I looked around the room to see if I could find the cooler. I'd researched the whole transplant ordeal, and learned that the transplanted organ is usually flown in and kept on ice in a cooler. *On ice in a cooler like a six-pack of beer?*

Again, it was too late to be worried about minor details. Thankfully the newly administered drugs relaxed me to the point that my mind wasn't going haywire. The drugs were diluting my latest nightmare. In a few minutes my chest would in fact be sawed and cracked open. At this point, all I could do was pray to GOD. I was reminded of the poem "Footprints," by Mary Stevenson. It's the one where GOD puts you on His back and carries you across the sand, leaving only one set of footprints. This moment I prayed the hardest. I truly surrendered, and believed that GOD would help guide the medical people to pull me through. The nurse told me to take my left arm, raise it with my palm up, and put it on a special section of the operating table—imagine a chalked-out police sketch. I recall the nurse saying, "You're going to feel really relaxed, so start counting backwards from one hundred." I believe I got to ninety-six.

The *Awakening* 14

"Mr. Smith, can you hear me?" "Good! On the count of three, I need you to cough, and then blow out through your mouth as hard as you can. Now, one, two, three blow!" (Cough)... With the cough, out came this strange apparatus I later learned was a breathing tube to assist in keeping me alive. Like being reborn, I took my first breaths on my own. Prior to the nurse's voice, everything was a blur. I knew I had been in and out of consciousness in what felt more like a dream. At some point, I heard voices, faintly saw figures, but what finally made me realize I wasn't dreaming was when I glanced at the Yankees on TV. Derek Jeter was up at bat. I murmured, "What's the score?" This of course let Nikki know that I was indeed back. Nikki's aunt and uncle were there, and one said something about the Pope's visit to New York, and that "the mob" had something to do with his visit. Unexpectedly, I jumped into the conversation by saying, "I am in no way going to comment negatively about the Pope or any other man of GOD after traveling where I just came from." They, of course, laughed at what they thought was my usual joking manner. There would be no LOL, I was dead serious, pun intended.

Although I had been heavily sedated, I had faint memories of seeing my son KJ and my stepmom Senora being in the room, along with several nurses. A memory that was much clearer was Nikki moisturizing my lips and wiping down my face—as we had discussed by the elevator one time. The day had finally come. I was the patient being wheeled around with the fifty or so drips running into my unconscious body. Many hours earlier I'm sure I appeared lifeless, but Nikki kept her word, and made sure I looked as alive as possible. I guess I'll keep my vanity all the way to the grave.

Although I was really groggy, I wanted to ask Nikki all the particulars of the surgery. *How long did it take? Were there any complications? How bad was my own heart, and what did it look like? We were talking about an organ I had been born with, and now it was where, in the garbage? Or maybe it was in a lab jar?* I needed answers, but as much as I wanted to talk, it was hard to stay awake. I was supposed to be unconscious for an entire day. I was told the surgery lasted from 3 to 7 a.m., and I was already trying to come out of it by midday, so they gave me more drugs to induce sleep. At about 4 p.m., I was trying to wake again. I couldn't stay asleep. I was probably thinking, miracle performed—*Rise and shine!* The doctors and nurses gave up, and allowed me to wake slowly on my own in time for the Yankee game.

The more conscious I became, the more the vast pain struck, like I had been in a terrible car accident. Three tubes, one of them large enough for a garden hose were coming from my body. The catheter in my penis wasn't comfortable either. Also there was a three-inch apparatus in my neck that allowed all the various drips and drugs to enter directly into my blood stream to balance out the functions of my original organs with my newest one—the heart of a twenty-one-year old. As important as all the drugs were to my recovery, I was truly fond of only one: Dilaudin, which was at my fingertips. It is in the morphine family, so you can see how someone can become accustomed to a powerful pain medicine. I was good for a "hit" every 12 minutes. I understand how that sounds, but when your chest cavity has been sawed in half, cracked open, and your heart has been yanked out, it has a tendency to cause a little discomfort. With this said, it didn't really matter if I was a temporary drug addict or not. The pain was manageable, but mentally I knew what I'd been through physically, and didn't want to imagine the pain without the medication. I'd always been told to stay ahead of the pain.

Initially I couldn't feel all the tubes and drips, but that all changes once you become more conscious. The mind is unbelievable. However, following surgery I ended up with a friend that would be dependable for life. Transplant patients all receive teddy bears called Cough Buddies. These are used to apply pressure to the chest cavity in case you cough, so you don't rip apart your stitches or damage the permanent wiring. I slept with my bear; nicknamed CB, nearby, and still do to this day. He serves as a reminder of when I lay there afraid to cough, and when a sudden cough came about, his fluffy body provided protection. After surgery, patients develop a lot of fluid that has to be coughed up to clear the lungs. CB helped me get through some tough times so I became pretty loyal to him. I now understand why children grow dependent on their stuffed animals. At the time, I was totally okay with that.

The second night after surgery I received a bed bath, including the essential banging on my back to loosen the phlegm. This was when I finally got to see my tubes and all the bruising my body had taken. This was somewhat disturbing; I looked so very weak and skinny. Senora and Nikki said how beautiful my skin looked because my color was back. At first I thought they were crazy. I was a black man. I never thought my color left. Now I could see I looked different; I had grown so accustomed to how I had looked. I had blood everywhere—it felt unbelievable. I could hear my new heart beating. All of this was a little scary because it was new territory or it was new "old" territory. It would take some getting used to, but I was up for the challenge.

We take the little things for granted when we're blessed with a "good" heart. Prior to surgery, I had sat in a heart transplant support group listening to other recipients share things that I couldn't understand. Things like my color coming back had really mystified me, but now I was living proof—I could see it. Always a person with great veins, after surgery they were full and very blue green. Capillaries in my legs and feet that had caved in due to lack of circulation were now full. My fingertips were pulsating, as was the back of my neck and behind my ears. This was the direct result of my new heart's ability to immensely increase my blood flow. Now having a twenty-one-year-old's healthy heart brought my ejection fraction (EF) into an appropriate range for the first time in many years. As my doctor once told me, "You have no idea how bad you truly are since you've been sick for such a long time." At this point, I really loved being able to hear my heart beat, and everything else that came with it.

Post-surgery, my appetite was unbelievable. I couldn't stay full. Before I went insane, the nurses finally told me why—one word: prednisone. I was on an extremely large dosage of this steroid, which makes you want to eat small people. It's an important immunosuppressant that causes several different side effects. The hunger thing was a big one for me. It also can cause moodiness and make your mind play tricks on you. Fifteen minutes after the nurse gave me the first dose I was aware of, I thought for sure the tiles in the ceiling were moving. The square air vent also began to look like the Roman Parthenon. Everybody in the room laughed as I transformed into a temporary lunatic. The liquid diet I was on wasn't working for me, but I understood why. And just the thought of having to get out of bed was traumatizing, together with the notion of going to the bathroom, the idea was completely unnerving. My whole body was still sore; the thought of any unnecessary straining made me feel faint. I couldn't get that porterhouse steak I'd been wanting for three months out of my head. But I guess the Jell-O and ice cream would have to suffice.

I found the Coronary Care Unit (CCU) wasn't so bad. The nurses were incredible. Whatever courses they'd taken for bedside manner served them well. My post-transplant nurse was amazing. She might have been the nicest human being I've ever met. As if her job depended on it, she made me feel totally comfortable. If you thought you couldn't do something, she assured you that you could. I felt like I was a project she would be graded on, and if I wasn't provided for properly, the she would ultimately flunk. At any rate, whatever she was making salary-wise was much too low.

Two days later, the most grossly underpaid employee walked into my room—my surgeon. Dr. Samuels was a young stud of a surgeon, under forty years old, I believe. I had never met him before (conscious, anyway), but when he walked in the room, I knew he was someone very important. His "swagger meter" was through the roof! He emitted a certain confidence that I'd never seen before. I liked this guy. All of that was before he told me that he was the "mechanic." Mechanic was a proper term because he, like a lot of the surgeons, was so adept at his craft. At Columbia Hospital, they swapped organs out like engines. In less than a four-hour surgery, he'd led his team in and out, ending with another new heart transplanted. For the most part, the patient's surgeon depended largely on who was on call at that particular time.

I believe that GOD brought the two of us together. Of course, others will say it was mere coincidence. The fact that he was a young man who shot straight from the hip was right up my alley. When he first entered the room, he told me who he was, and then said, "What the hell was that in your chest?" I asked him, "What do you mean?" he continued on to tell me that my old heart was "a piece of shit." (Tell me how you really feel, Doc). He said it was large, stiff and scarred. He also informed me that I hadn't had a lot of miles left on it, but this new twenty-one-year-old's heart was going to make me feel unbelievable. I was dumbfounded and speechless. I knew I was bad but I never thought I was that bad. Without him stating the obvious, I knew I probably would have died within months without a heart transplant. He assured me I was now in great shape and the only problem I'd had was no longer a problem. A surgeon with his directness and honesty was definitely the type I needed.

I was now a new man because of my faith, a great surgeon and surgical team, and last, but not least, my angel of a donor. I had a long road of recovery ahead of me, and I owed it to my donor and his family to see it through. I was led to believe the hard part was over, and as I clutched CB, my teddy bear, I was determined to one day leave this hospital forever, grateful to those who'd saved my life.

Moving On Up

Not long after surgery, actually two days later, I was moved from the CCU to the Cardiac Intensive Care Unit (CICU), which now meant I had my own room, and not a curtained-off area. This room's flat screen TV was even better than my first one. Grab a new heart, and you catch an upgrade. I liked the improved perks already. I could see construction workers building the hospital's new cardiology wing outside my window but the view didn't matter much anymore. I was going home soon. To be honest, it could have been a brick wall. The most important thing missing was the infamous clock in my old room. This was sort of ironic, because time didn't matter now. The clock in my old room should have been a calendar since I stayed there for months. I was going down the home stretch.

As the nurse practitioner Maria had told me, I watched the garden across the street go from snow-covered to blooming beautifully with different combinations of colorful flowers. I watched the construction workers in cut-off tee shirts. I wanted to wear my cut-off tee shirt, skinny little arms and all. It didn't matter that I was so skinny from weight loss and months of being sedentary. I dreamed of normalcy. My day was coming soon. I was doing so well after surgery that they reduced one of my many vital medicines because my body matched my donor heart. so well. Later it was determined this was done a bit prematurely because all of a sudden my blood pressure was higher than normal and I had problems with my sugar. "Sugar," for many people, especially people of color, is associated with being a diabetic. Diabetes did run on both sides of my family, but it had never been a problem for me. They explained all of these things were in direct correlation to the transplant, and would probably subside. Organ transplantation is a balancing act. My sympathies went out to all of the diabetics because I was now getting my finger pricked every odd hour. Thankfully this only lasted a week until my levels went back to normal. The doctors scrambled to adjust my medications so I could move closer to being released. Again I was told because I had been in such good shape my body was responding very well. Now I was happy that I pushed myself to walk or work out, even when I truly had no desire. Three days after the surgery, and I still had two tubes in my midsection and that same annoying Frankenstein-like unit hanging out of my neck. The I.V. in my arm fed the other medicines, but the most uncomfortable thing hanging from my body was the catheter. For obvious reasons, I was extremely happy when they pulled it out. Boy, do we take going to the bathroom on our own for granted. On the side of my bed was a bag that received the blood and other fluids draining from my chest cavity. The bag was gravity-fed, and early on, it had to be emptied many times. As days went by, the blood and fluid began to diminish, and changed in color from red to light pink. The three tubes were removed, leaving only the one in my neck because it was the most vital. It was the most efficient and effective way to administer the immunosuppressants. Any slippage on these drugs would result in a good possibility of my body might reject the new heart. After five days post-surgery, I still hadn't gotten out of the bed. I was growing anxious—and numb.

I had an incredibly cool male nurse who catered to my needs as if we were family. He really knew his job, and unfortunately I left some dirty things for him to do. It was embarrassing, and I'd constantly apologize, but Nurse Anton didn't flinch. He insisted it was his job, and admired me for not looking like someone who very recently had had a heart transplant. I wasn't sure what that meant, but I took it as a compliment. He made sure I had my shaving supplies, as well as hot water to wash myself. He also gave me total privacy when I was able to use the bathroom by myself. Although that sounds easy, it was not. This was a mighty task because I was hooked up to a machine with about five feet of play between the leads on my body and the machine, which I called "the leash." The toilet bowl was about five feet away, and I had to be very cunning to get to it, plus sit down and not be discovered. All patients were monitored, and a camera watched our every move. So with only a couple inches to spare, I had to simultaneously maneuver the curtain and sit down. It took me about seven days to move my bowels and become a "regular" guy. This scared me, but my doctors told me not to worry, and said for me to imagine my body as an empty water hose that was slowly being filled. Basically, my digestive system was empty. Anton was around to help me with many things. Luckily, he was there when it was finally time to stand up. I felt awkward, but he helped me steady myself on my weak, atrophied legs. I never imagined standing would present such a task. I was like a little child, except everything about me was adult. I was now the new toddler, and it was a weird, proud feeling. The process of being reborn left me with an exuberant glow, I was beginning to feel magnificent.

As my pain started to subside, I began to get antsy, wanting to go home, getting ready to fly from the comfortable nest of the hospital. The day was soon approaching when I would have to test my new heart without the comfort of a nurse or doctor coming to my rescue. That was a scary feeling, but I was up to it. Sometimes I forgot my hospital was an actual teaching hospital, with students coming and going. Then I would hear the whispers of the current doctors telling the future doctors my situation. I was so tired of being a science project. It's not that I got my new heart and wanted to bail out, but as a patient, you get tired of being looked at as *something* rather than *someone*. I was ready to be one of "them" again. I wanted to be regular. I suppose it was somewhat bosh to think I'd ever be regular again. I carried the heart of another person in my body. I was grateful to be alive, but I began to think I was a freak show. In this world, if you look to your left; then to your right, how many people would you see who have someone else's organ in them? Sometimes being looked at felt funny. I wanted to show the folks in the lab coats I was like them—that anyone of them could be laying here. I'd taken care of my body. I ate well, exercised and never would have thought I would be in this position. The most valuable lesson learned was that heart disease doesn't discriminate. *So don't snicker*, I thought, *this could be you one day*. I also went to college for science, but chose to not go to med school. That was a choice, getting heart disease was not. I didn't fit the likely profile. *Check my records Mr. Lab Coat; you'll see I was a regular person like you. Don't you see my great muscle tone?*

Let's blame that little tantrum on prednisone. I was totally grateful, and felt I was chosen to be a heart patient for some peculiar reason. It had to be the medication, because it wasn't in my nature to act that way. Med students were part of the elite, as was my surgeon and his grossly underpaid team. They didn't look down on me. I knew that. Peering out my window at the sleeveless workers, I thought, "I want to go home." Maybe I wasn't a med student or even a construction worker, but I had a purpose in this world. I wanted to get out and prove myself once again.

The Professionals

In order to truly serve the health profession well, I think you have to be a smart, caring, and compassionate individual. From blood techs to nurses to doctors, you should really love your job because in this profession you deal with people's lives.

In many occupations in the world, if a worker has a bad night on the job, he/she might tend to take their frustrations out on the customer. In the hospital, workers are health professionals and the customers are patients. When I was a teenager, I worked at a nursing home, even though I partied all night, I still managed to make it to work at six each morning. As a young man, I didn't totally understand the whole "patient's rights" thing. I mean, I wasn't a bad worker or disrespectful, but looking back I'm sure I was less patient and sympathetic to my older clients' needs than I would be today. First, I was young and immature, and second, I was hung over.

Neither reason was in the best interest of the client. As I became older and wiser, I knew I needed to put my client first. As I watched my grandparents aging, and I was able to put myself in an older person's shoes, I prayed that one day I would be blessed enough to get to be their age. We are not promised tomorrow, becoming old is definitely a blessing. I desired to become a walking, talking history book, and share things with my future grandchildren. Laptops, cell phones, social networks came about in my era, and I yearned to live to see more miraculous inventions.

One observation I made while in the hospital was that too many times, the health care profession didn't switch shoes with the patient. For instance, a blood tech came into my room each morning to draw blood. First I'd hear her high heels, then the light would go on, next she would talk loudly to someone in the hallway, and of course, she'd jab me with the "painless" prick, Maybe it was me being insensitive to her working all night, or her getting ready to work a full day or maybe, or maybe, it was her sensitivity issues. The fact that I had been a captive of my bed for such a long time, all the while with a cloudy fate, made me a bit edgy. The blood tech didn't know I had to take Ambien every night and woke up intermittently, or GOD forbid, if I did start to sleep soundly, the Lasix would make me go to the bathroom in between naps. Obviously, she didn't know these things, but I was tempted to ask if she ever took a course on bedside manner. I believe in being sexy, but who the heck wears high heels on an overnight shift? When the bells and whistles weren't going off, there was a rare quietness on the hospital floor. Those shoes would tend to break that up in a hurry. Maybe I was a little too tough on her because I was in a hospital. As a patient, I yearned for a good night's sleep which would elude me for me months.

About five days after the miracle, I'd been told I would be getting out of the bed to take a walk. This was a very scary time because when you've been so close to death, and now you have another person's heart in your body, you're not sure if it's going to allow you to do more than simply lie in bed. For five nights I'd laid in the bed with all kinds of machines monitoring my new heart, lungs, blood pressure, and breathing. Throughout the night in CICU, all you heard were bells, whistles, and alarms. My own monitor went off a few times because of things like sudden movements or shallow breathing. Even the thought of walking raised my anxiety level and increased the rate of my breathing, so to actually do it left me with a mixed bag of feelings. As afraid as I was, I knew taking these steps was going to get me closer to leaving the hospital, and getting my life back. I recalled how disappointed I was on that important fifth day, that instead of the nurses "walking me," I had to settle for only getting out of bed. At the time I didn't understand what the big deal was. It was only standing up to sit down. Soon I found out why it was such a big deal. It took three nurses to help me to my feet. They found it to be pretty funny that I almost toppled over. The rush of blood was unbelievable. I almost fainted. Obviously the nurses knew this was a possibility, that's why there were three of them.

Day six was another day of just sitting up. Finally day seven came. I was totally prepared for it by now. My wife was there with my new Nike sneakers. My son KJ, the ball player, was there to witness this great feat. In order to begin, I had to be hooked up to a portable breathing monitor, and also an electrocardiogram machine to constantly check my pulse and heart rate. Now all the bells and whistles would be coming with me for the walk. It was time to test this new puppy out. As I prepared for the journey, I felt somewhat like a toddler taking their first steps—but I was a forty-five-year-old man with a new twenty-one-year-old heart. In preparation, I shaved and attempted to look like new money walking out of my quarters. Again, it was game time, and I treated this event the same way. I had new sneakers, and a brand new set of hospital pajamas. I decided a sweatband would be overkill. I thought of this as my debut for all those near the nurses' station. When a heart transplant patient begins to walk, it's a sign of becoming more acclimated to society. I was ready, swollen ankles and all. This was the first time I'd worn sneakers in a long time, and they felt great, albeit tight. As we walked around the nurses' station and past the other patients' rooms, I heard many folks applaud. This surprised me because I didn't think it was that big a deal to the nurses and doctors. I was wrong. These people saw my success as a personal accomplishment. This is what they did for a living. No one had ever applauded me at my job, but I actually felt I should be clapping for them. Every lap around the nurse's station was parade like, and I was getting really giddy. The nurse was having a hard time keeping up with me. She thought I was walking too fast, but I attributed this to two things. The first one I call the Forrest Gump Syndrome, like in the movie when he broke out of his leg braces, and simply ran like there was no tomorrow. Second, my nurse was only about 4'2", with very short legs. My wife cried. Hell, I cried. KJ poked fun at me, saying my gait was horrible. I reminded him that so was his at fourteen months. This was new for me—again. My vital signs remained normal. My legs were very weak from the atrophy that had set in, and my hip joints hurt from lack of movement. My ankles were still swelling as my body continued to adjust to the new medications and to the vastly improved circulation. The nurse asked me if I wanted to continue after the third lap, but I told her no. I knew I had a tendency to overdo things, and this was a major step. I'm sure this was the ex-athlete in me, but I didn't want to set off any of my alarms. The tears that trickled down my face were caused by the fact that I knew the battle in the hospital was drawing to a close. Once upon a time, walking normally seemed like a distant dream, and here I was walking—and best of all, I was breathing easily.

An interesting twist came the next evening before walk number two. I was ready to double the amount of laps, but first came a rude surprise. A different nurse was assigned to me that night. She appeared to be an experienced professional, and initially I had no issues with her. All this was soon to change as she prepared everything for my venture. I was ready to go, and as I pulled out those new Nike sneakers, her whole expression changed as she peered down at my beautiful blue and white Air Maxes. "New Nikes?" Beaming with pride, I said, "Brand new!" She said, "You can't wear those." I laughed because I thought she was kidding. Looking down at her shoes, I thought the joke was because my sneakers were so much nicer than hers. I continued to lace them up until she made me realize she was very serious. Her statement, "We don't do Nikes," took me briefly to a place I'd only heard about. I thought about the sweatshops in Asia where women and kids labored at well below minimum wages. The people were basically treated as slaves. The fact that my nurse was from the Philippines helped me draw the conclusion she was indeed serious. This was something dear to her, and she wasn't going to let it go. I tried to be compassionate towards her feelings, but I was a patient, for GOD's sake! Soon there would be another patient for her to tend to, but on this evening—it was me. All I wanted to do was take a walk. Obviously she didn't know that when you serve the public the customer is always right. With great dismay, I unlaced my Nike's and put on my hospital-issued socks with the rubber matting on the bottom. Needless to say, this walk wasn't as enjoyable as the first had been, but as the saying goes, I had bigger fish to fry. I'm sure her boss would not have agreed with her thought process, but not wanting to cause a problem, I walked with pride. Neither this nurse nor a pair of sneakers was going to hold me back from my ultimate goal of leaving the hospital. After my walk, instead of stewing about the nurse with no compassion, I thought about healthy folks instead.

Months earlier I lay in my room and listened as a man across the hall coughed and gagged to clear his throat all through the night. For a while, I fell into the trap with some of the less-compassionate nurses who shook their heads, wishing he would stop this annoying sound. He made me want to go shake the hell out of him. A few nurses believed he was "performing" on purpose. I did, too, until I thought back even farther. I used to *be* that guy. One time in a Red Lobster restaurant, I had a slow, constant coughing attack. At that time, all I wanted to do was to clear my throat. I couldn't, and it was frustrating. It was a nagging, persistent cough that made me feel like I had an egg yolk caught halfway down my throat. Foolishly, I tried to wash it down with a margarita, and then some water. This didn't work so I took a cold-and-sinus pill. This also didn't work. Thirty minutes later, it went away, but I could only imagine how embarrassed Nikki felt as everyone looked at us to see if I was all right. Closer to my admittance to the hospital, I would lay on the couch with four pillows, taking more cold medicine and drinking tea. Denial is an absurdly crazy thing. I continued to attribute my congestion to having a cold. I'm sure my daughter was embarrassed as well when she would have friends over, and I'd have an awful coughing spell. De'Asia would come downstairs and ask was I all right, and I'd reply, "Yes, but I have a bad cold." That would be the explanation she gave her friends as she turned up her music in order to drown out my coughing. The truth was that my heart was beginning to give out. It wasn't pumping well, which was causing the other organs to be starved of blood. Fluid was building up in my body, hence the term "congestive heart failure."

Now when I sit in Starbucks and hear an older person continuously coughing, I am empathetic. When I'm at the movies, and the person in the next row can't stop clearing her throat, I'm more compassionate. All you have to do is think for one moment. Do you really believe people want to have nagging, aggressive coughs that everyone can hear? I don't think so. Sometimes all it takes is a little common sense, mixed with a bit of compassion. I wish the nurses would have thought of that and treated that man across the hall better.

Pack Your Bags

17

Nights in the CICU were long, and at times, scary. I'd already had my surgery, but others were very ill, and awaited their fate. A few were there because of complications from a previous transplant. The only thing I could think of was getting out of the hospital. It sounded selfish, but I came for a specific purpose, and now that my wish was granted. I wanted to resume my life. But I knew I had to take a tentative approach. Things were going too slow, and I was ready for more physical challenges. After being in the CICU, a heart-transplant patient is usually transferred to a regular hospital floor, which is called a "step down." This floor was much less intensive, and was designed to prepare the patient for discharge.

Unfortunately, no beds were immediately available in step down, so I was stuck in CICU for eight more days. During this extended stay, I became stronger and healthier as my body and new heart were getting used to working together. The healthier I got, the more I realized how sick the people were around me. I heard constant moaning and groaning from patients in so much pain. I recalled being sick enough to have numerous blackouts, but I was never in the outward discomfort like they were. I felt sorry for my neighboring CICU patients. During these eight days, at least two people died, having succumbed to the evils of heart disease. I thought to myself, *I can't let this break my great spirits, even though I am surrounded by sickness and death.* I sympathized because I knew a little over a week ago, I was one of them, but now I really had to get out of there.

To help me combat these feelings was Mr. Jones, a patient who was waiting for his second heart transplant. He also needed a kidney, but this man's positive outlook put mine to shame. Mr. Jones was a black man about my age, and had his transplant ten years ago. He became a mentor to me, and I leaned on him with silly and not-so-silly questions. I considered anyone who had already been down this road an expert. We'd sit for hours like professor and student, and I took in all of his knowledge.

In this, his second stint, Mr. Jones had a rare blood type, and had been in the hospital for almost a year. We never really discussed why he needed another transplant so soon. To me, ten years was soon—but I later found out this was about the average length of heart transplants.* Mr. Jones cautioned me to eat right, drink plenty of water, exercise often, and not to party. The fact he stressed these things made me curious. Maybe he hadn't been strict enough on himself about these things? Either way, I never asked him because I felt he was in a situation that didn't need any additional stress. Mr. Jones, the heart transplant veteran, walked me through a lot of things, and as with a lot of my co-patients, we formed a tight bond.

(Survival rates are: Year 1=88% in males / 86.2% in females, Year 3=73% and 69% respectively, with the longest survivor living for 31 years–and dying of cancer in 2009.)

Finally, one early morning, they came to move me to step-down floor. This was a fantastic feeling as the nurses gathered all of my items and cleared out my room. I shared my new room, but this was a minor detail. The fact that I had a room with a bathroom door was in itself a great plus. The leash was off my neck, and I no longer felt like a little puppy dog. Because all my monitors were disconnected, I was free to move about freely. This felt a little weird. Mainly because in almost three months, I'd always had some form of monitor to constantly gauge how my heart or vitals were doing. No more warning bells, cameras and nurses running to my rescue. These were uncharted waters. Also, walking to the bathroom was new, and I laughed to myself because it was normal to the staff, but to me, the new-heart guy, it was exhilarating. When I was able to be alone in the bathroom, I examined myself in the mirror. It always scared the living crap out of me as my face looked puffy and "chipmunk-like." I had only seen glimpses of my face since surgery, and never saw it while standing, but I quickly attributed this look to the steroid I was taking. I had always heard prednisone could give you "moon face," but I never expected to see mine in full solar eclipse. I looked downright scary. I prayed my face would get back to normal—and eventually it did. As I looked at myself from head to toe in the mirror, I was really, really thin, no more muscles, literally just skin and bones. It was almost as if someone had deflated me. My self-exam was nearly over, but I saved the best for last. I slowly removed my chest bandage, and stared at my body's most recent scar. As far as permanent scars go, it wasn't so bad. I was determined to wear it as my badge of courage, faith, and commitment to GOD. I wouldn't need a heavy necklace to bear a cross because I would treat this as my chain. It would serve as the ultimate reminder of everything I went through, and would always make me aware I'd never be one hundred percent normal. This scar would tell my uplifting story of being lucky—and also being a medical marvel. Staring in the mirror, I mentally prepared myself for the time when everyone would stare. It was inevitable, and told myself I would be fine with people passing judgment about a battle they could only imagine.

Physical therapists came in to work with me. As I started to walk up and down the hallways, my legs began to get stronger. My body was coming together as one again. A day into step-down, I was moved again, but this time into a room that overlooked the Hudson River. I had a magnificent view of all the boats and people enjoying the spring weather. I yearned to be outside again, and get some fresh air. I knew my time was coming, and it was coming fast.

All the people I originally befriended early on, who needed transplants, had now received them. Some of us had smooth rides, and a couple like myself, had no complications at all. The main reason it took me so long to get discharged was because of the lack of bed space in step-down, or I might have broken the record for the quickest discharge. Because I was complication free, I had mixed emotions about my discharge. The hospital was my security blanket, and I'd grown accustomed to all the monitoring. Things were moving too smoothly. Something had to go wrong because I was doing too well. As Nikki and I were enjoying one evening watching all the action on the river, the medication coordinating nurse, Nia came into tell me that I was going home tomorrow. "Did she say tomorrow?" My breathing rate increased. Nia was great, but that announcement almost caused me to choke to death on my food. She said the last major thing I had to do was learn my medications. Nia really stressed how vital it was to know how and when to take them. She had spoken of this at a support group, and explained again how this was vital to my health with not much room for error. A transplant patient's medications, especially the immunosuppressants, are his/her lifeline. This would be a small price to pay for receiving a new life, and would be as easy as brushing my teeth each day.

Nia told us she'd be back at midday the next day with everything I needed. Nikki and I were extremely happy, but not uncontrollably, because we'd prepared for this day. It was finally going to happen.

Nikki left early to go shopping to buy her newly skinny husband something to wear home. I was left to myself one last night. I floated around the hospital floor, saying my good-byes to certain people, and I visited Mr. Rich, who received his transplant a week before me, but had some minor complications. I left him some reading material, autographed photos of my brother and son, along with my phone number. I retreated to my room and closed myself inside. Prior to taking my nightly dose of Ambien, I had to do something one last time. I got down on my knees and prayed to GOD. I thanked Him for the blessings, and asked Him to continue to bless me. I thanked Him for bringing me through all the long, and lonely nights, and how He made it all worth it. With His help, first and foremost, I had made it. I prayed for the wonderful doctors like Drs. Maxwell and Samuels, who, together with their staff, saved my life. I thanked the Lord for my angel donor and his family for making a decision that changed my life. It was because of him I had another chance. So many nights I wasn't certain I'd wake, but each morning I was still there. Tonight was the last night of my ordeal. I went from overlooking a garden in the winter, to overlooking the scenic river in the spring. GOD always took care of me.

Morning came and Nikki and De'Asia were there bright and early. I could tell Nikki was excited by the different outfits she'd brought me. She was a professional shopper anyway, so whenever you gave her a reason to shop, she was the best, hands down. I came into the hospital wearing a double extra large, and now I was barely a large. Originally I was 250 pounds, but on this day, I was a paltry 163 pounds. Now, I was more of an extra medium, I joked. My waist went from a forty to a size thirty-four. We laughed, but it was all good. I threw on a new baggy sweat suit that engulfed me, but I once again felt like a million bucks. My feet weren't swelling anymore, which caused my size twelve sneakers to feel loose. Wearing two pair of socks quickly solved the problem.

Nurse Nia came in with a big paper bag containing more than thirty different medications. She had everything we needed: a pill cutter, a seven-day pillbox, blood pressure machine, thermometer, and all kinds of paperwork and schedules to familiarize me with my meds. She was quite thorough, and the absolute best at her job. After another lesson in pill taking, we all hugged as she wished me the best. The last thing I said to her was to not be surprised if I called her if I got confused, and she responded, "Anytime." The discharge nurse finally came, and after signing the paperwork, off we went. She asked if I needed a wheelchair but I bellowed, "No way!" I walked in, and now I was walking out, hospital mask and all.

As we got down to the lobby, De'Asia and I waited as Nikki went to get the truck. The heck with my vanity, I was just happy to be leaving the hospital. It didn't matter that the "normal" people stared at the man with the mask—I was a free man. I felt myself getting a little emotional as I stepped outside into the warm spring air. Finally, I had fresh air, and it was almost overwhelming—a far cry from the stagnant air inside the hospital. It was something I hadn't experienced for three months so I had to take small sniffs; I even had to step back inside for a moment. The truck pulled up and Nikki reminded me to get in the back. De'Asia got a kick out of that because she got to ride shotgun. We drove off, leaving the hospital in the rearview mirror. My wife's driving normally makes me nervous, and now the medications intensified the feeling. I reminded her not to shock my heart too soon, so. We all laughed hysterically, as we always had, when I said, "Please don't scare the heck out of me today."

As we proceeded across the George Washington Bridge, I sat in the back seat of my own truck with tears wetting my hospital mask. Of course my daughter laughed at me because she didn't know the many weeks I had stared at the bridge, wondering if I'd ever be going back home. Today I was, hospital rested and battle tested. My old, sick life was left in the dust, and I was riding home a new man. Somewhere in a large petri dish, I imagined my damaged 45-year-old heart. Now because of a young donor and his family, I was able to resume a new, healthier life. I would forever be indebted to this individual, and vowed not to let his death be in vain. I prayed that he was in heaven. I wanted to meet his family someday to show them that his unfortunate passing did in fact help a good person. Today though, I was going home, and through my tears, I knew everything was going to be all right.

18
Free at Last

When I arrived home, I received a tremendous surprise. The surprise was, there was no surprise. Nikki had honored my wishes. She knew I wasn't ready to be bombarded with a giant reception. Even though it wasn't what I wanted, I fully expected welcome-home signs, balloons, and a house full of folks. We were the party-planning duo, and I couldn't think of a better reason to have a gala event. But I was quite impressed that she listened, and I agreed she could do a party later.

Having been cooped up in one room for so long, our apartment felt much bigger. Nikki and De'Asia both watched me as I gingerly walked around surveying our home like it was a new mansion. This was a day I had dreamed about.

Eating my own cooking again was also a major part of my dreams as well. I knew I had to be on a low- fat, low-sodium, and low-cholesterol diet, which really wasn't that different than the way I'd eaten in recent years anyway. I'd always been the cook in my adult life, so I was excited about getting back to feeding people and making them smile. All the years of watching Grandma cook really paid off. More importantly, I was ready to prepare healthy meals a little differently than those in the hospital. We'd arrived home about three in the afternoon, and I immediately jumped into making dinner—baked chicken, rice, tossed salad, and dinner rolls. I suspect this gave Nikki the impression that she was off dinner duty for the rest of our marriage. It really wouldn't have mattered, because I was just happy to be back home, doing what I'd always done.

Later as I lay on the couch basking in the surroundings, I realized that my chest was beginning to hurt, due to all the moving and twisting I'd done that day—especially the cooking. It had obviously been awhile since I'd taken pain meds, and my body was a bit shocked. I popped two Percocet pills, and soon I was feeling no pain. Pain pills are amazing; it's great not to feel pain. When I fainted from the arrhythmia and had broken my ankle, I had to wean myself off the pills so I definitely understood how many folks become dependent on them. Not me, because I took them only when absolutely necessary.

Finally, came the moment of truth; it was shower time. Can you imagine not being able to take a shower for three months? Granted, I'd taken bed baths frequently, but to actually have water flow continuously all over my body was another dream come true. I carefully climbed in the shower, and although I was only able to let the water pour over me from the back, I found this renewed experience to be unreal. As the saying goes, "You don't miss something until it's gone." I showered until the water ran cold. Remnants of iodine solution were still coming off of me. As I dried off, I was already thinking about the next day's shower.

As I stepped out of the shower and looked into the mirror, again I stared at my frail body. I uncovered my bandages and saw my eight-inch scar, which resembled a zipper. I also had two holes from the drainage tubes that had hung from my mid-section. I took this time to thank GOD that my catheter didn't cause any damage to my "you know what." It had been so uncomfortable that I thought for sure there would be a problem. My legs, which were never my strongest feature, looked like toothpicks, and my butt was flush with my thighs. Shoulders that were once broad were so sharp they looked like I could inadvertently stab someone. My face was emaciated, but my eyes were filled with the promise of a better future. The only positive feature was that I had my six-pack abs back. I recalled KJ joking with me, "Of course, because you only weigh a 100 damn pounds!" I replied to this "dream killer" of a son, I actually weighed 163 pounds. All of this didn't matter. I saw the mirror as an ally, and not an enemy. It reminded me that although slight in stature, I was indeed alive.

Now it was time to realize my final dream for this long day—to sleep in my own bed. I climbed into the super king with my cough-buddy teddy bear, and sank into the tranquility of the mattress. Prior to drifting off to sleep I prayed The Lord's Prayer. I thanked the GOD for seeing me through this day, and for granting me my wish of coming home to my family a healthier man. I vowed to be a better man. I asked Him to continue to watch over me, and keep others strong. It then dawned on me, the last time in my bed I prayed for the Lord to please allow me to wake. I didn't include that in this prayer, I finally felt confident I would be there in the morning. After such a long journey, I clutched C.B. and thought about how fearless I finally felt about going to sleep. I smiled and drifted off into my first deep sleep, with no bells, whistles and alarms, in my own bed, in my own home.

Waking up in my bed, I was filled with gratitude, because it felt great to not have nurses taking vital signs or the breakfast truck coming at 7:30 a.m. like clockwork. I was now able to go downstairs and make my own healthy, protein-rich meal. I'm sure the hospital kitchen staff meant well, but I didn't miss their food. I was determined to get my weight up, so I ate a lot. The prednisone steroid dose was up to 15 milligrams twice a day, making my appetite surreal, so it was important to implement healthy meals. Peanut-butter sandwiches, crackers, and nuts, especially almonds, were a big part of my diet because of the calorie content. I became the smoothie king with bananas, blueberries, strawberries, yogurt and two percent milk. Fresh salads with lots of chicken, baked fish, vegetables, and turkey, to name a few, became staples in my diet. I ate much like this before, but now I was much more strict because I wanted to make sure I did everything right to protect my new heart. I did notice one change though. My taste buds were a bit different. I suddenly I found myself liking sweets. I was never a big sweets guy like my brother Bo, but now red velvet cake became a major favorite. Ice cream, M&Ms, and Snickers were just a few treats that I came to relish as delicacies. I tried to eat them in moderation, but I blamed the medications for my weakness.

Initially I was on approximately fifty pills a day, which I took, without chewing, as if they were a handful of Skittles. There were the big three immunosuppressants: Cyclosporine, Cellcept, and the aforementioned prednisone. The rest were vitamins and supplements not necessarily essential, but definitely helpful in maintaining my new life. Some of the other side effects were tough to deal with, but not to the point of making me suicidal. The Cyclosporine made me grow hair at an alarming rate. It seemed as though I'd shave one side of my face, and then go to the opposite side, and by the time I was done, the first side needed to be shaved again. It also made my face, head, and neck oily. The Cellcept made me shaky and unsteady, and also gave me a nervous feeling that made me pace back and forth. It also made me forgetful. The adjustment was trying at times. In the beginning, it was laughable, but I began to wonder if this was how it would always be.

But even with all of these side effects, my life was returning to normal. I started out taking small walks around my block. Initially, I walked slowly for fifteen minutes, eventually increasing to forty-five minutes at a more rapid pace. In the midst of my walks, I took in my surroundings like the flowers, the pond, the ducks, and the birds. I felt ashamed to have taken the simple things, like nature, for granted. As I continued walking, my heavy breathing caused my incision to pulsate with pain. I knew it was part of the healing, so I didn't worry. At first, Nikki walked with me, but weeks later she reluctantly allowed me to walk alone. Halfway through my walk, she would call me on my cell to receive an update. I loved walking alone because now I could really focus on my surroundings, and give thanks for my blessings. I was able to walk down by the river or stop down by the Little League games and watch kids play. Ironically, it was the same field I played on when my heart troubles were nonexistent. My new heart was affording me the many pleasures I had sometimes taken for granted.

One day after being home, it was time to get back to my outside life. Nikki had to drive me, so I was at her mercy, although she allowed me to make a few stops. The first one was to my primary doctor who made the initial assessment of a potential heart issue. He hugged me so hard he almost broke my aching sternum. I understood his elation though, because he had been there from day one. He had also watched me go from a young man with hardly any health concerns, to someone with a colossal health issue. Dr. Samuels was genuinely happy for me. Afterwards, we were off to my job, and since it just happened to be payday, I figured I'd pick up my own check. My boss was shocked. He was so excited that I had to apply a firm stiff arm between us because after all, it was just only fourteen days since the transplant. I was still a little too fragile to go inside to see everyone else, but they understood. Our next stop was one I'll never forget. For the last three months, I'd been relegated to hospital pants or gowns so I had no real need for money, but now with jeans on, I felt the need to "fluff" my pockets. It had been so long I almost forgot I was able to carry money. I signed my check and gave it to Nikki to go handle the transaction. She peered back like I was crazy, as if to say, "Get your butt out of this car and handle your own business." She was right though, because I was home, and it was time to start fending for myself again. The truth was I was sort of afraid, the medication was making me feel a little weird. I had always been in control, and now my vanity was affecting me again. I didn't feel totally "normal" yet. As I walked into the bank, I got confused about how much to deposit, and I couldn't figure out how much I wanted to receive back. My hands were shaking as I filled out the deposit slip, and I felt as though everyone was watching me. The medicines were doing a job on me. Frustrated, I gave up, and just deposited my entire check. Dejectedly, I walked back to the car to be met by Nikki asking if I was okay. I explained to her what had just happened. I became very emotional because I didn't feel like myself. I questioned my new life asking myself, "Was this it?" Was this how it would always be? Something as simple as going to the bank was now a big deal.

Nikki reminded me that it had only been two weeks, and certain medication's side effects were in full force, because my dose was still high. She was right that I was being way too hard on myself. I had expected more, but I was forced to believe that as meds were reduced, and I had more time getting acclimated to everyday life, things would get better. I eased out of the car, and went to the ATM machine to make a withdrawal from the amount I had deposited minutes earlier. We both laughed.

My errands were done, and now it was Nikki's turn, so off we went to the first of two hair salons. Why two salons I don't know, I was only a passenger. I soon learned that I was hot news. Coming from a small town, everyone seemed to have heard about me being sick. While sitting in the salon, I looked around as I heard someone's cell phone ringing out of control. I thought to myself, "Answer the damn thing already." That's when I realized that it was mine. I'd totally forgotten what it was like to have a phone. My phone had always been an extension of my hands. A voice on the other end asked me if I was all right. I explained to my friend Yvonne that I certainly was. She stuttered trying to tell me that her friend saw me, and said I looked sick. "I mean incredibly thin," she clarified. I laughed and replied, "No, I'm quite well, thanks." Obviously it must have hit her, because she asked, "Oh, wow, did you have your surgery?" I answered, "Absolutely, and it went very well. By the way, how is your dad?" I immediately took the focus off myself because I knew her dad was sick, and this gave her a way out of the awkward conversation. She told me he was fine. I excused myself and hung up.

This would be the first of many weird encounters. The rumor mill was alive and kicking; the worst rumor being that I had died. At this moment however, I sat among all these women, proud to be in the same salons that my wife had braved alone for three months with many folks asking her questions and being afraid for her. I was now a walking example of what strong faith and medical science can do. My brother Bo came by to give me a break from "salon day," and took me by his job. He showed me off to his new co-worker like a new car. By now I understood how proud my family was, which showed me how frightened they must have been. As I waited for him outside a deli, I got out my lunch bag and had my own little snack. It was around noon so I popped my meds, and continued to wait in the back seat. Bo drove me back, and Nikki was done, so we went home to conclude my first official day out. I made dinner, and later that evening, we took the first of what would become many evening walks.

Of course, the second day home also began with a memorable story. We went to our neighborhood grocery store where we ran into a gym buddy and his wife. His reaction was, "Wow, Smitty, what the hell happened to you?" I thought perhaps the fact that I had a breathing mask around my neck might have a prompted a softer approach. As Nikki frowned, I proceeded to explain what the last three months of my life had been like. This was the same guy who suggested I take steroids to get bigger in the gym. Obviously ignorant, I chose to skip the explanation of my old heart problems. As we walked away, I called out to him, "See you in the gym soon." I'm sure he didn't believe this. His approach was all-wrong, but it prompted Nikki and me to turn to each other and say simultaneously, "People are different." This was our new motto. We would have handled that situation totally differently because we were more compassionate people.

It wasn't until the next day that a true epiphany came at one my favorite places, the movies. I had always viewed the movies as my two-hour safe haven. Now, a few rows away, a man was repeatedly sneezing. With nurse Nia in my head, and Nikki giving me "the look," I pulled my mask over my face. If this was the worst it was going to get, then I would be fine. As I sat back and enjoyed my lightly buttered popcorn, I again reflected on my journey. This was a current scene from my own life's movie that I couldn't have envisioned at all only weeks ago, but here I was, doing what I did best. While in the hospital, I actually ran through all of my DVD collection, so I would find myself thirsting for a good movie, and here I was. I thought about my other heart patient friends and what they might be doing. I prayed they were doing as well as I was. I longed to see them again, minus the hospital's bells and whistles. My life was truly worth living, and although I knew that everything was great right now, I wasn't naive enough to think there would never be another bump or bruise. At this point though, it didn't matter to me because I couldn't see that far and I wouldn't allow myself to look negatively into the future. All I knew was that today was a good day, and I was happy to be home, and happy my movie popcorn still tasted the same.

Battling heart disease, and finally receiving a new one, taught me many wonderful things. One of the major things was that it was impossible for me to expect compassion out of everyone, when, by nature, so many people focus on the negative. I mean seriously, most headlines are about bad news. Prior to my ordeal, I'd be the first person to pick up the newspaper if the front page read, "Earthquake kills 20,000." The paper with, "Woman donates 5 million to cancer research," would be left on the newsstand. One more thing I've incorporated into my life rules is to never, ever judge a book by its cover. Don't rush to a conclusion, based on someone's appearance.

We scheduled a family trip, which I cleared with my doctor at my one-month check-up after coming home. I felt it was important to let my family in the South know I was all right. They had called many times to check on me. I'm sure things got misconstrued about my health. It's like playing a game of telephone tag—when a story starts out one way, but ends up another way. It was my duty to stop the negative press, by letting everyone see me for him or herself, especially since I was the first in my family to have a transplant. I knew I couldn't educate everyone, but I wanted to give my family first-hand knowledge of the whole donor/transplant process. Of course my grandmother was first on my list. We surprised the family as my mom and aunt lived there as well. It was a great couple of days as everyone asked questions, and I answered them. My cousin Carter was there. He was like my brother, and although he'd led a troublesome life at times, he seemed very concerned about me. Like me, he is an emotional man, with a great presence when he's on the right path.

While in Virginia, we picked up my 12-year-old daughter Kelsey, who is the youngest of my children. She was shielded the most for obvious reasons. She has always lived with her mom in Virginia, and was about three when my problems kicked off. She was a daddy's girl, and not until I had to, did I explain what was going on. She, of course, had no fear that anything bad would have happened to her dad. A straight "A" student since pre-k, the obvious things became harder to hide later on. Kelsey was concerned with one thing and one thing only, her dad's muscles. Kelsey has always loved her dad's muscles. If I ever slowed up at the gym, she'd be on me, "Dad, your arms are shrinking." "Dad, your chest is getting smaller." "Hey Dad, what's up with those abs, I don't know, I think you're getting a little flabby." With Kelsey, I could always tell if I was in good or bad shape. A mirror truly wasn't necessary. She never knew she was my undercover personal trainer, without ever taking a course. Unbeknownst to her, she whipped my butt into fierce shape. Getting out of bed on those rainy days, I had to go to the gym because I needed her approval. Furthermore I was trying to mask the obvious: I was a sick dad. The analogy that I'd come to use was, what good is having a Bentley if the engine is bad? Kelsey didn't realize I had a bad engine. All I was doing was waxing, polishing, and putting a shine on the exterior. As my illness required, I found myself explaining little by little, different battle wounds, such as cardio version burn marks left on my chest by paddles used to jump my heart back into its normal rhythm. I'd had to explain to Kelsey why the hospital personnel were defacing her dad's body. When we'd traveled, Kelsey would wait patiently on the other side of the airport x-ray screening booth, while I was searched because of my pacemaker. She'd joke, "Hey, was that fun?"

The worse things got, the more I shielded her. I'd even forced myself to go down to Virginia to her basketball games when I should have stayed home, close to my doctors. I had to go. No way could I miss her birthdays and different events due to my heart's failure. I mean, after all, I was the strongest person in the world to her. If she was to become the first female president, I had to let her know nothing can stop a person from doing what she wants or must do.

Anticipating what my daughter was going to say about her "new" dad, I wondered: *Would I get her approval?* Yes, I would. She was very excited to see me. She had fun with my very-pronounced six-pack stomach, although she wasn't too happy about my muscle-less arms. I could live with her assessment. I took her words and actions as a passing grade. She wouldn't learn until later in life how seriously ill I was. All in all, the Virginia visit was an extremely happy time, and I took pride in showing my grandmother my new scar. We had matching pacemaker incisions, so I let her know that I'd finally won the battle of the scars, she was happy to concede. After manning my usual position at the grill, we ate. Then we were off to North Carolina to surprise my stepmom Senora, who had been by my side at different intervals during my hospital stay. I could always count on her and I needed to see her, because she was as close as I could get to my late father, I wanted her to see how I was coming along. Senora scheduled a small barbeque so all the family could come to me, and I wouldn't have to visit to a thousand different houses. It was another great time, almost movie-worthy. I felt the love and gave it right back.

The majority of family said they prayed for me, and I'd always reply, "Thank you, I received them all." My illness was hard on my dad's brother, my uncle Bill. He was very emotional whenever he called the hospital, and no matter how hard he tried, he'd always cry at the end. I believe it was because my father was his best friend, and looking at me reminded him of his brother. I loved this guy, and I wanted him to know I was all right. The trip ended well, and the only slight wrinkle came on my way home. A long-time female acquaintance texted me and said she hoped I felt better since she heard I was very ill. I replied, "Thank you, but I'm doing extremely great." She said, "Okay, I'm glad you're making yourself think you feel great." I had no response—I wasn't going to allow one piece of negativity disrupt an entire great trip. Furthermore, she wasn't family, and I promised myself I wouldn't feed a fire. Again it was probably someone who had seen the somewhat-shrunken me, and had assumed the worst. At this time, I was cool with this perception because after all, I had had a heart transplant one month ago, and was much closer to being great than I was to being sick.

We wrapped up our "world tour" and returned home to New York. Weeks later, Nikki finally got to throw her bash. She put together her own welcome-home barbeque, which was fantastic, especially when she surprised me with a few unexpected guests. Maria, the transplant coordinator, and her son Ike, a great football fan, made the trip from upstate New York. They had a fabulous time, especially when Ike had his football signed by my brother Keith, who was then playing on Ike's favorite team, the Tennessee Titans. The biggest surprise of the day was Dr. Maxwell, my cardiologist— my star player. The man had saved my life and made the right call when things got bad. I finally got to meet his wife and kids, and although I didn't want to embarrass him, I had to let them know how great he was at what he did. As usual, he shrugged it off, and instead told me how great I was, consistently deflecting any credit, as usual. The barbeque with family, friends, and co-workers, turned out to be terrific. This event officially told me it was time to start getting back into the mainstream.

Getting Back to Normal

At my first organ-donor awareness walk, someone said I would eventually start to feel normal again. It was 17 days post-transplant, and I talked about my excessive hair growth, unbelievable appetite, shaky hands, oily skin, etc. The other organ recipients replied that this, too, would pass. Eventually it did, and I pressed forward to get back to normal.

It had been awhile since I'd been behind the wheel of a car, and I was a little apprehensive, with lingering emotions about driving. The medications still made me jumpy, plus I was concerned about the city traffic.

However, I had a bigger concern. I was en route to the hospital for a biopsy. All the transplant patients will tell you this procedure is really the worst part of having a new organ. The running joke among the transplant team is, although they'll give you a heart, they slowly take it back one piece at a time. The procedure only took thirty minutes from preparation to end. My palms sweat every time I thought about something going into my jugular vein and into my heart to check pressures and pull out at least four small pieces of the heart. As I drove down the parkway, my minded drifted towards the dreaded, upcoming procedure.

Although my mental state was a bit unstable, it felt so good to be driving again. I hadn't driven in six months, but like riding a bike, things felt natural right away. I had my truck washed the previous day, and I watched its reflection on the guardrails. Quickly this beautiful morning turned ugly, as I heard a police siren, and automatically, I said out loud, "I guess the truck is too shiny." I knew he was coming for me. As expected, the officer pulled me over, and from my personal experience and from watching TV shows, I knew to abide by every single rule. Furthermore, being late for my all-important day at the hospital wasn't an option, so I didn't want to be detained for anything extra. The officer informed me that I was being pulled over for tinted windows, and driving eleven miles over the speed limit. He took my license and returned to ask me about an old fifty-eight dollar parking ticket in Jersey from 1997. He asked me if I knew anything about it. I replied, "No." He then asked if I had fifty-eight dollars, to which I replied, "Yes." I was then told to get out of the car, prompting the feeling that this simple traffic infraction was now taking a turn for the worse. This is when I proceeded to use an excuse I thought was pretty valid.

Politely, I informed the officer I was a recent heart transplant recipient. Next to me on the seat were all my meds, including my giant bible-like heart transplant book with the words *Heart Transplant* emblazoned on the front. I also let him know I had to get my blood drawn before 10 a.m. Through all my explanations, the officer still insisted I get out of the car and step to the back. I realized now I was going to be arrested for an old fifty-eight dollar ticket that I knew nothing about. I pleaded one last time as he checked my pockets, and asked me to put my hands behind my back. Finally, I was beginning to lose my patience because my kindness and heart transplant "excuse" weren't working. I asked him was he prepared to take on this responsibility, and repeated how time sensitive my situation was. It was now about 8:45, and I was panicking. I wasn't sure how my chest would hold up with my hands cuffed behind my back, sitting in the backseat of a police car. I was about to find out as he said he was fine with taking the responsibility for me potentially missing my blood work and my 10 o'clock meds. He was obviously fine with taking a chance on my healing chest as he cuffed me and put me in the police cruiser. He searched my whole vehicle, and then locked it. The only smart thing he did was to grab my lunch bag with my medication.

No way can I explain how humiliated and angry I felt as we zoomed to the police station five minutes away. I question the officer's sensitivity training, especially since I had every bit of proof that I was telling the truth. We arrived at the police station where he un-cuffed me. I gave the clerk sixty dollars, and told her to keep the change because they, of course, had none. Eventually, I was returned to my truck on the side of the highway, and made it to the hospital right before 10am. When I explained the whole debacle to the nurse practitioner and my doctor, both somehow found it hilarious. It wasn't until a while later that I saw some humor in the situation. However, neither of them had ever been a black man, nor been arrested for something so petty. I guess they viewed it as a simple detention. For me, it was a panic situation. Little did they know I hadn't been sure I'd ever see the light of day again. I asked my doctor to watch more news on TV.

At this particular check-up, four months post-surgery, my doctor became so encouraged by my progress that she signed off on me going back to work. I had no complications, and most importantly, no signs of rejection with the new heart. My body was slowly adapting to the fifty-plus pills a day, and the doctor lowered the dosages, including the prednisone.

I felt as though I was creeping closer to normalcy. The fast walking turned into jogging and soon, running. This time when I went to KJ's football game in Miami, I was feeling terrific. Of course, this visit didn't go without a hiccup. As I sat there soaking up the beautiful Miami air, I once again reflected on my journey. Sitting among 50,000 fans, I wondered how many had been down a similar tumultuous road, and survived to see their loved one play this game. Not long after that thought had crossed my mind, I noticed the play had stopped at the two minute mark because of an injured player on the field. In preseason NFL games, 80 players are on each roster. So out of all 160 players, it was my son that went down with a season-ending injury. I was mortified, wondering: Did I bring bad luck to my son? I felt like I was once again in a dream. One of the worst feelings in the world is for something to happen to your child—when you can do nothing to help. As two giant men helped carry my kid off the field, I was reminded my kid was also one of these giant men.

Later, KJ would show me how intelligent he really was when I saw him limping towards me outside the locker room with a brace on his left leg. I asked him, "What's up?" He then replied, "They're saying ACL (anterior cruciate ligament), but all I could think about as I laid on the ground was, it's my knee. It's not like I'll need heart surgery." With that statement alone, I knew my son had arrived. Life finally threw him his curveball. I was proud of him, and knew after this setback, he'd be a stronger person, physically and mentally.

In addition to my primary career, I also own a mobile car detailing business. When I was getting sick, all I could do was sit back and watch my employees do the work. I recalled trying to bend down to put on tire shine only to have my oxygen supply cut off. Of course, now I know this was my enlarged liver pressing against my lungs. For me, waxing a car eventually became extremely tiring. Any extra exertion put a strain on my weakening heart. The longer I had my new heart, the easier these things became.

I could now run my business as a more hands-on boss by doing most of the work myself. My son, Jared, became my right-hand man, and it became more of a father-son business, giving us many bonding moments we had previously missed out on because of my illness. I was happy to have my son beside me talking and laughing as I taught him the business. It appeared Jared was very happy to have his dad back. This was the same dad who had not been able to play ball in the driveway with him or even feel up to a walk in the mall.

Getting back to normal meant making the gym my safe haven once again. On my triumphant return to the place my journey began, I cautiously approached the same elliptical machine that had served as a bucking bronco the infamous day my defibrillator first fired, saving my life. I felt the need to get back on it, to prove it hadn't beaten me. It hadn't. The elliptical was no problem anymore. I incorporated a cardio workout, along with weight training, and I watched my body slowly transform. My chest began to poke out again as well as my butt, arms, legs, and shoulders. Everything started to come together as it once had been, and I now felt comfortable returning to work. I knew that most people didn't go back so soon, and having an abundance of sick time built up, I could have stayed out for four more months. But I have always had some kind of job since my paper route at age twelve, so working is all I know, and it makes me feel whole. Sitting around collecting checks isn't my thing. Plus I was tired of feeling like a "sick person."

So, on September 1, 2008, ironically Labor Day, I went back to work. Prior to being hospitalized, this day was a vacation day. Naturally, I cancelled it because I surely didn't need vacation—I needed to work. I wanted to work. Although some of the medications still had me feeling a little weird at times, they wouldn't prohibit me from fulfilling my job duties. Everybody welcomed me back, and it was business as usual. I immediately jumped back to grabbing a bunch of overtime. It seemed as if the planets were lining up perfectly with my world returning to normal. I had my health, family, and job. All three of these essentials combined to make me feel complete. Remove any one of these and it would offset my equilibrium. Other heart patients thought I was crazy not only to go back so soon, but to go back to work at all. I saw *THAT* as crazy, because I was only forty-five, felt great, and was able-bodied. Why not go back to work? Retirement was simply not an option. In a matter of four months after my heart transplant, I was back to doing almost all the things I liked. Traveling, weightlifting, and sporting events were substituted for hospital rooms, fainting spells, and IVs. Life was good again, and I was determined to prove to everyone I was in fact, back to normal.

Biopsy: The Necessary Evil

When we were young and we got sick, my grandmother would say, "Oh don't worry, baby, you gonna be all right, go get the Robitussin." From a cold to a broken leg, Robitussin was the all-faithful cure. Although it was funny, we called that a "backwoods-home remedy." Grandma wasn't the only family member to over-medicate my brothers and me. My father would sometimes give us a choice when we'd do something objectionable. Choice one was a spanking. The other option was castor oil. To this day, I'm still not sure why castor oil was an option for punishment. If you've ever tasted it, then you understand why my butt hurt from the spankings. The punishments were cruel, although at times, necessary.

I'm sure I speak for all transplant patients who share my thoughts on one particularly cruel procedure: The Biopsy. Again I'll say that in life, most people might see one thing as unjust, whereas others will view it as necessary. The biopsy happens to be both. Early on it was hard to imagine it truly being necessary.

Of the hundred or so procedures and operations, the heart-muscle biopsy has always made me the most nervous. Notice I didn't say it was the most painful. The most-painful title still belongs to the pelvic bone biopsy, but that was a one-time deal that actually caused tears to roll down my cheeks. Angioplasty, cardio versions, catherizations, defibrillator implantations, ablations, neurological biopsies, MUGA echocardiograms, to name a few, didn't compare to the queasy feeling I'd always get prior to a heart muscle biopsy. In fact, during some of those procedures, I actually chose to be heavily sedated.

Being wide-awake for the first biopsy was all it took. This happened in the late stages of my heart failure, which I'm positive is what enabled my doctor to conclude I had restrictive cardiomyopathy. The strange thing about some invasive procedures is that the extremely smart hospital personnel face the monitors toward the patient. I don't understand that. I recall my first angioplasty (which is similar to the Rotor Rooter drain clearing). The doctor fished through my arteries with such precision, and after finding no blockages, asked me "Wasn't that amazing? Did you watch it?" Happy it was over, I replied, "Doc, I would have much rather watched ESPN." The whole O.R. team erupted with laughter. What I was saying, in essence, was, "What the hell! Turn the monitor away or put me under!" I'm sure some "sick" patients like watching their life in the hands of others, but not me. This was the beginning of many procedures I would have the option to watch on the monitor—or not.

As I sat in the waiting area for today's appointment, the wife of a new transplant patient asked me why I was there. I politely told her for the same reason her husband was. She looked bewildered, possibly because I was twenty years younger than her husband. I reminded her that heart disease didn't discriminate. Because I had about 30 minutes before my dreaded procedure, it gave me time to once again reflect:

December 5, 2003 was the date when my heart was first invaded. This once uninhibited organ of power and grace would now be subjected to prods, pokes, dices, and cuts. It was suggested to me that because my heart kept jumping out of rhythm after various attempts at cardio versions, it was now time for a pacemaker. It might help me tremendously. At the time I was ready to try anything because I could barely breathe. Even watching people walk uphill tired me out. It would be as simple as going in the heart to burn (a process called ablation) an electrical synapse permanently, and then add leads from a pacemaker that would slow my heart rate. Sounds confusing? I thought so too, but I learned to trust my doctors. I was, after all, their MVP (Most Valuable Patient), or so I thought. Doctors are pretty doggone cunning to make you think you're their favorite. This worked for me though. Thankfully anesthesia was used for this procedure. All went well with my first cut and adding the lump in my chest.

When it was finally that time to take replace the pacemaker with the defibrillator, there were a few issues. This unit was a bit larger and this time I wouldn't be sedated, but I was made comfortable. Enter the TV monitor once again. I figured, what the hell, I'll watch the screen, because this would be an easy one since the leads were already inside my heart. A local anesthetic was administered, as well as medicine to make me drowsy. I felt a lot of pressure as they re-cut my initial three-inch scar to remove the first unit. I heard snipping and the occasional, "You okay, Mr. Smith?" The problem arose when it felt as though they tried to force a four-inch unit in the original three-inch incision. They pushed and pushed as I watched the monitor. After approximately twenty minutes, I noticed the monitor was getting fuzzy. It didn't take long for me to realize that this was due to tears in my eyes. Somewhere along the lines the doctors penetrated the damn pain button. As they tugged, the pain grew exponentially. Again they asked if I was okay, and I said yes. *I'm such a liar,* I thought. To be honest, I thought that I was supposed to feel pain. I had no idea I was to let them know the numbing medicine had worn off. I was sure that they would know little stuff like that. Actually I thought the tears would be a dead giveaway. Finally, they were done, and later when we discussed it, they told me how crazy I'd been. Little did they know, I thought *they* were the crazy ones. After at least twelve years of post-graduate school, they couldn't tell that the anesthesia was wearing off? The tears in my eyes didn't give it away? Was I crazy? Yes, I was, and I vowed right then and there to never try to be the tough guy again. Doctors and health professionals from here on out would know whenever this patient had a little pain. The key word here was *pain*. Biopsies didn't hurt that much but it was hard to get used to them because of nature of the procedure.

Today was clinic day, plus biopsy. That meant I'd see Dr. Fanning, my post-transplant doctor, as well as receive a biopsy. For the patient, it starts the night before at 10 p.m. We take our immunosuppressants, and can't eat or drink anything after midnight. This is to ensure that eleven and a half hours later, our residual levels are in a decent range, and the medications don't have to be tweaked. After the blood draw at 9:30 a.m., it's off to have an X-ray and an EKG to make sure the heart is anatomically correct and performing in rhythm. The next two events can flip-flop, pending on scheduling, but I'll save the best for last. The visit with your post-transplant doctor is a simple exam of temperature, blood pressure, weight, etc. It's a pretty basic physical, giving the patient the opportunity to explain any developments, new or otherwise. This is the appropriate time to talk about your meds causing erectile dysfunction, back pain, or mild arthritis in your hip. The exam takes all of about ten minutes, yet it probably costs my insurance about three hundred dollars. It usually ends the same way. Doc: "You feel great?" Me: "Yes." Doc: "Well, you're the best; keep doing what you're doing." (Cha ching goes the cash register). Part of my doctor being able to make such a strong statement was based on the findings of the endomyocardial biopsy (two thousand insurance dollars, by the way).

The Biopsy schedule was as followed: Post Heart Transplant = Four consecutive weeks; Next three months = every other week; Next four months = monthly; Next three months = every other month; Annual exam on month twelve. The biopsies become less frequent after the annual exam because the first year is the most important, a sort of probationary period for your new heart.

Usually, I took a book to read or my IPod Touch to listen to music in order to remove "the edge." There's no other way to describe the waiting period other than filled with nervous energy. As you sit outside the clinic doors, every thirty minutes another patient comes out, and it becomes apparent that your nightmare is closer to becoming reality. The absolute best part, if you can imagine there is one, about the whole procedure is Donna, the nurse in charge. Everyone that has anything to do with cardiac care in the hospital knows Donna. To me, she's the clinic's biggest asset, because she has good old-fashioned values, which make sure the patient comes first, and is comfortable as can be. Eventually, she comes with papers to sign. I call them "the just-in-case papers." You sign these papers in four places to exempt the hospital from any wrong doing in case things go horribly wrong. I thought, *who in his right mind reads all of that crap?* Even if you did read all of the fine print, it's not as if you'd cancel the necessary procedure. So as usual, I roll the dice. With my first heart, I signed my life away so many times that I don't think twice about signing hospital papers. Donna strokes my shoulders as I'm whisked away to a room. Off comes my shirt, and out comes my pride as the doctor and Donna tell me how muscular I've become. They really know how to set the mood.

The biopsy is the most definitive way to show rejection, so the degree of rejection or lack thereof, can determine whether or not your doctor will alter your schedule. As I climb on the table and begin to get prepped, my palms begin to moisten. Donna, ever the professional, notices a change in me, so she pats the back of my hand as she simultaneously puts on the blood pressure cuff. After so many biopsies, I've come to have favorite doctors, and less favorite ones. Today I have one of my favorites, Dr. Jensen, who says he's a great football fan, and how he loves it when they hit home runs. Thankfully, he's a much better doctor than football fan.

Dr. J makes small talk as he sterilizes the right side of my neck, and then stings it a few times with the Lidocaine. Next comes pressure from putting the sheath in my vein. This is like a very small tube that will enable the other apparatus to more easily enter my vein and heart. The mood is very upbeat with everything moving relatively fast, barring unforeseen problems, such as not being able to get around a nodule or scar tissue. The fishing expedition now begins as Dr. J feeds a line down the sheath into my heart chambers to check the internal pressures. With Donna holding my sweaty hands, I feel nothing. But if I feel adventurous, I may glance up at the monitor from time to time. I hear them bark out the numbers, which doesn't mean a whole lot, but the main thing I hear is Donna saying, "Excellent." Out with the old, and in with the new, as the bioptome (the instrument used to clip out parts of your heart for sampling) is introduced. This new "fishing line" is a sterile, stainless steel wire with two cloth pin-like pinchers at the end. It is inserted in the sheath, and carefully guided down into the heart to grab four to six dandruff-sized pieces of heart muscle.

At this point my palms are dripping and I'm not the least bit embarrassed because I'm scared as hell and don't have the time to fake it. I have no idea what Dr. J and Donna are talking about because I'm praying long and hard and I refuse to lose focus. I can't be concerned with the fact that Dr. J has switched bioptomes, because he can't get a proper bend to get a good "hit". The proper bend is similar to trying to use a hanger to unlock a car door. The closer he comes to pinching a piece of heart; it feels like my heart might jump out on the floor. It races as Donna calls out "beats," and then he snips. I relax until the next three snips. Finally, I hear "we're done," which is incredible music to my ears. Donna pats my hand as Dr. J starts to withdraw everything, and closes me up while keeping constant pressure on my jugular vein. The doctor puts on gauze, and I'm sent on my way. Thirty minutes from beginning to end doesn't sound too bad. Of course, this was a non-eventful biopsy. Occasionally you get another doctor who can't find your vein, and punctures capillaries all around your neck, making you look like you're back in high school with massive hickies. Or you might get another doctor who doesn't apply enough pressure, but gives you a bandage and sends you on your way. After you put on your white shirt, walking past all the cute nurses on your way out, you realize that your whole shirt is bloodied, making it hard to be cute. It's kind of similar to smiling at people, and later looking in a mirror only to realize that you have a fat piece of blueberry skin from a smoothie in between your teeth. Excuse me, I digress. Finally, there's a doctor who's relatively new at the biopsy game. She takes a sample, and you jump a foot off the table. She innocently asks, "You felt that?" With a tear in my eye, I reply, "Yes, a little." Nurse Donna knows to schedule me for a date when that doctor is not on duty.

Biopsies are brutal, and I'm sure I speak for everyone when I say I pray there will come a time when a simple blood test will be able to conclude whether or not you're in rejection. New studies exist, such as Allomap, which does this, but all the evidence is not in yet. Therefore, the good old-fashioned biopsy remains that necessary evil.

The biopsied samples are sent to an outside lab so the doctor doesn't get the results until the next day. I found the nurse practitioner to be the cardiologist's right-hand person, and he or she calls to inform the patient of the results. During the twenty-four hour waiting period, the patient is hoping to hear two distinct words: "No Rejection." Then the stress from the procedure is totally over. The biopsy is still the quickest, most efficient way to tell if your body is rejecting the new heart. Certain levels of rejection let the doctor identify to adjust your medications. Usually a hospital stay and prednisone boost is enough to get you out of rejection mode. So as much as I despise the whole biopsy ordeal, I appreciate its effectiveness. As I continued living my life, Dr. Fanning insisted I not worry about the medical side, such as biopsy results. She assured me my medical team is adept at adjusting medications, should a rejection occur. I trust her because this is her livelihood, and she came highly recommended.

Most people, outside of my situation, never understand what it is truly like to live on borrowed time. To them, it's simply a doctor's appointment or procedure, but to the transplant recipient, it's a vital concept. As bad as I detest the biopsy, I know it's the best way to discover that my life's not in danger.

The Choice Is Yours

Months after my transplant, I saw a friend in the grocery store. My defenses went up as usual, however, she never batted an eye at my very slim weight. She gave me a robust hello and asked how I was, saying she had heard rumblings on the street about me being very sick. She questioned how I did it. I assumed she meant how I kept my illness a secret, plus made it through the tough times.

I knew Beth was a deeply spiritual woman, so I reminded her how great GOD is. I also told her my options were slim at the time. She did make me think however, if I'd chosen option A over option B, where my life would be. Living with heart failure, or more specifically restrictive cardiomyopathy, simply didn't seem like the better choice. Her approach was very tender, and I appreciated her gentleness. I soon found out, however, she may have had a subliminal reason for her extra concern because she too, had a form of cardiomyopathy, and was extremely frightened about her future. It was about a year after that initial meeting when she reached out to talk to me about her doctor's findings. She had been told she might have to go on the transplant list. Like most of us, she was having a hard time grasping that incredible prognosis. I told her how she'd come to the right place for a comforting opinion.

Who in their right mind would say, "I need a heart transplant, but it's no big deal, because it's going to improve my life." My guess would be not many people—it *is* a very big deal. A transplant is not fail proof, and it's certainly not a cure. From the onset of the harrowing news, it's a huge hill to climb, but it is conquerable.

People like Beth often descend deep into a depressed state. You feel alone everyday, like no one understands your problem. Most people immediately think about their family like, "What will happen to my kids or my ailing grandmother if something happens to me?" The concept of living is more difficult to imagine.

A heart transplant is the final option to heart failure, and by nature, when we hear "final" we think "the end." In the early moments of discussion, you don't perceive it to be the end of suffering from heart failure, although, in reality that is the result of a heart transplant. Those ugly days of feeling like you don't want to live anymore suddenly vanish. At least, that's the message I try to convey to Beth and others in her predicament. Through the generosity of a donor, your new life begins again after receiving a transplant. Now when I speak to people waiting for surgery, I pass along information I didn't fully understand at the time.

I give patients benefit of my firsthand experience, because as a transplant patient myself, it's easier for them to believe someone who's been through it. I try and break things down as simply as possible. I make Beth and others understand they need to walk when they don't feel like walking, exercise when they barely feel like moving at all. I now understand how doing this definitely makes everything that much easier post-transplant. Strengthening everything around your weakest link can make you feel more peaceful and secure as you ease back into everyday life. If you compare your body to that of a car, it becomes clearer. My body was that of any older car with bad head gaskets and rings. It was replaced with an engine with very low miles. In theory, the wheels may fall off, the body may rust, but with the proper care, the engine can run for a very long time. With a proper diet and exercise program, I can stay away from potential problems. Friends may joke with me about the "rabbit food," I eat—vegetables and fruit, but at the end of the day, I feel better and less sluggish than having eaten a steak, which I still do occasionally. The 5:45 a.m. gym workout prior to my workday is essential, including three miles of cardio. Now, of course, every heart transplant patient will not keep such a regimented schedule, nor is it mandatory, but personally, I vividly recall the depths of hell I've encountered and I plan to delay any return trips as long as possible.

As sure as the sun will rise, I will have episodes. When I speak to others, I don't pretend to be at 100 percent all the time, but I do tell them I feel 100 percent better. I sincerely believe that some of the drugs I take are responsible for certain new physical symptoms. I developed osteoporosis in my hips, a rise in my bad cholesterol, and easy bruising, to name a few. Luckily, there are more drugs can help fight these flare-ups. It basically comes down to a trade-off. In the beginning I had one giant problem, but now occasionally I have smaller ones. It's a trade that I'll accept each and every time.

Occasionally because of the previously mentioned episodes or flare-ups, I find myself speaking to an organ recipient. Once it was Paul, who was beginning to have a constant cough again. I reminded him to watch his diet, and curb his sodium intake, as we were all taught. Kayla, who had been doing so well but would get high rejection levels every so often, was the most difficult. She was in and out of the hospital, but remained upbeat. Her latest problem was that antibodies had gotten in her bloodstream because of another rejection, and her blood had to be cleaned. I tried to stay positive because she needed me and everyone else to be in the fight with her. The truth is I didn't know how much more she could take. However, we organ transplant recipients are a resilient bunch. Kayla may waver a bit, but she gets right back on course, and does what she needs to do.

When I look in the faces of other potential transplant patients, I see fear, which is natural, of course. It's a relatively new medical marvel. The first successful heart transplant was in 1967 *(It was in Cape Town, South Africa by Dr. Christian Barnard, which makes the process a little over forty-years old. I have spoken to a couple of recipients twenty years removed from surgery, which substantiates how far we've come since Dr. Barnard's first patient, Louis Washansky, who only lived 18 days).*

I feel it's my job to show potential recipients how good life can be by letting them see me talking about my own journey, and stating the facts. Not that I'm that much different than the other patients, but I definitely stick to the program. Our daily meds are our lifeline, and that's a priority second to NONE. The medical world has come so far. Important immunosuppressants such as Cyclosporine have been introduced, and are vital to thwarting rejection. Nurse practitioner Maria told me about a patient who traveled from New York to Boston to hang with some friends for the weekend, but forgot his meds two different times. He eventually died from severe rejection. Unfortunately, his priorities were all screwed up. Knowing some patients are still ticking (pun intended) after twenty years, plus new ever-changing technology, gives me all the hope in the world about setting the record for an organ recipient.

I told Beth I am a huge advocate of support groups because so many of us have the same anxieties and concerns. We are all afraid. This is one of the reasons I make myself totally available, and try to turn frowns to smiles, tears to laughter, doing my best to encourage the people who are waiting. Attitude is everything. Dr. Maxwell has asked me to talk to his current patients on the transplant list. I embrace my role, and it feels totally natural to give back in this way. I spoke of Dan, my mentor, in the support group when I was on the other side waiting. I feel like I am the new Dan. It was so unimaginable that I could slip back into looking and feeling like a "regular" person again. I don't resemble that old sick guy anymore, so it's important for me to let people see there's light at the end of the tunnel. It's normal for people like Beth to not understand how the whole thing works—I didn't. But you can find out what you need to know at support groups.

I sought out a support group twenty days after surgery because I needed even more knowledge from others who'd had their surgery. I was still grappling with my hands shaking, and uncontrolled hairgrowth. From attending previous meetings, I knew I would draw comfort, and also give my fellow sick people friends hope for a brighter tomorrow.

I had two choices. The first was being able to live as long as I could with heart failure, and the second was to get listed and receive a heart transplant. I obviously chose the latter, because to me it was inconceivable to continue my quickly debilitating degree of health. The first choice wasn't a viable option. I recalled the constant planning necessary to avoid around walking up stairs or inclines. The tired feeling that I'd grown accustomed to was getting worse. I felt like a guinea pig as I received different heart medications to deal with various side effects, like sensitive chest nipples or my battles with painful gout. I was living with congestion so bad that I practically chewed Lasix water pills like M&Ms, hoping to get my ankles to stop swelling. Also, the excess fluid, gave me a nagging cough caused by phlegm. Perhaps I could have lived with these complications. The key word here was "lived." I sincerely believe that I might have lived for one more year, maybe less, because my body was quickly breaking down. Specifically, my heart was becoming more and more stiff, like that old pink cracked rubber ball I played with as a kid. Timing was crucial. I could choose life or like an old video game, I'd need bonus play to extend the "virtual" game. With the potential of a new heart, I found the best way to win.

The vast majority of us don't listen to our bodies, and most will do what I used to do. I'd always push forward, ignoring the potential fatal signs. Like I said, "Pride will kill you." And it almost did indeed lead to my demise. How many times have you heard someone say he felt tingling in his arms with shortness of breath, and when he finally went to his doctor, he was immediately placed in the hospital? I know at least ten people who ended up having emergency bypass surgery because of blocked arteries.

I believe I was being incredibly ignorant. The way I saw it, I had been too healthy for so long. Lulled into thinking it was impossible for me to be sick; the old athlete in me wouldn't allow me to accept my fate. Trained to believe I was a well-oiled machine, I had to win by grinding it out. I attributed my congestion to a six-week cold. My excuse for the shortness of breath was that I was simply out of shape. I continued to duck the obvious fact that I was growing closer to either dying or needing a new heart. Having said that makes it simple to see how easy my choice really was.

Getting Back to Work

Living with the organ of another person certainly has its positives and negatives. Most recipients are extremely grateful, and life is much better than it was the year before surgery. Some of us question if we made the right decision, and can find it hard to deal with the restrictions and rules of transplant. The most difficult part has to do with the medications and their side effects. I've been thrown a few curve balls along the way.

After going back to work, I began to have problems with my left hip. The diagnosis began as an arthritic hip, resulting in a lot of physical therapy. Doctors had always mentioned that a patient's bone density could be compromised by some of the immunosuppresants, such as prednisone. Dr. Fanning weaned me off this steroid in a year's time. I continued to have trouble with the hip, but worked through it doing physical therapy, and using a chiropractor. There would be good, bad, and worse days. Similar to the pre-transplant days, I started to have restrictions, such as not being able to do cardio at the gym. The flashbacks became vivid once more. Impeding my gym workouts would seem to be counterproductive. I guess anything that slows or stops you from doing things you love to do, can be detrimental to growth. It became extremely difficult to put the hip pain behind me. I did actually put it behind me because the hip pain exacerbated my lower back pain. So as tasteless as that joke is, it was "behind" me.

I started to feel like a mess all over again. The guys at work would play basketball, and I had to stay on the sidelines. Imagine that, the most athletic person on the crew, and all I could do was watch. However, I was able to partake in the occasional dart game until I relinquished that activity due to boredom. My coworkers never realized that even as a competitor, I'd needed something a bit more physical.

I thought back over the twenty-three years I'd put in at the water company. I began my job as a twenty-five-year-old with a girlfriend and a four-year-old son, and had certain pride that I was the only one with a related science degree at the company. Although I didn't receive any extra benefits for higher education, I still chose this company over others because of the level of responsibility. I worked shifts, and 66 percent of the time, I was alone, directly in charge of drinking water for tens of thousands of people. The first thirteen years wasn't really physical. Handling 50 pound bags of chemicals and the occasional broken pump came easy, the hardest part being the constant shift work.

Eventually something started to go wrong. Of course, now I know it was the onset of heart disease. My job became physical as I began to labor up the twenty-five stairs. My boss Tim always asked, "You okay kid?" My usual answer would be that I was. For some absurd reason, I always thought, job first and health second. At times I'd go to work in a heavy snowstorm as my kids watched in amazement, knowing their dad would have to shovel snow at work, when I could barely walk through it without becoming exhausted. Sometimes I'd work 16-hour shifts on holidays so my bosses could stay home. The money was good, though. I became so accustomed to pushing my weak heart to the limit. One year we had a big flood, and I stayed at work for 31 hours straight. I started coming to work with my ankles and feet so swollen that I had to wear regular sneakers because my steel-toed boots would cut into my skin.

Christmas Eve 2007 I stopped at the mall to get my wife a gift before going to work at midnight for a double shift. That was quite a tall task because I couldn't walk thirty feet without taking a rest in between stores. The pair of sneakers I ended up buying wasn't the gift I really wanted to get her or the gift she truly wanted but they were at the last store where I had energy to shop—knowing I still had to go to work. In the wee hours of the morning, I crunched through the snow to grab my samples for testing, using those 30 feet as my breathing parameter. I'd stop to catch my breath before continuing walking. It's funny but that was the weakest time of my life, and I still worked the most overtime that year. I am also proud to say I was one of the few that called in sick the least often. I probably dragged my butt to work on many occasions when I shouldn't have.

After being back to work for three years, I decided to have my hip reexamined. It came with much reluctance, but the pain was too much too mask anymore. Osteoporosis had taken over, and not much room was left between the ball and socket, which even I was able to deduce from the x-rays. Another surgery meant being out of work again, which I detested. I think I saw this as being weak—which is pretty darn silly. It wasn't a life-threatening situation, but it would still be a long road back. Again, I found myself sitting around my home watching the New York Giants' tickertape parade after winning the Super Bowl. Four years before, I'd been lying on the couch, suffering severely from a failing heart. At least this time, I knew I could push myself hard with my physical therapist because my heart wasn't an issue. I had my hip resurfaced by one of the best orthopedics in New York. Hip resurfacing was a relatively new procedure. I was only out of work six weeks, but I should have taken another two because of an awkward limp that I still have. My scar was about twenty-four inches long, and its "L" shape ran from the middle of the side of my thigh to the middle of the left cheek of my butt. My hip socket was cleaned up, a metal piece was inserted, and the top of my femur was shaved with a metal ball inserted down a few inches.

I was starting to really feel like the bionic man, and my scars were becoming quite prominent. My hip surgeon seems to think my right hip may need to be done in a few years, but I'm not sitting around waiting for that. Like most others, I'm living day to day. But the major difference is I'm doing it with foreign body parts and man-made insertions. Many other patients might have retired from work. Not me. No way would I "take the money and run." In fact, I had no clue when I'd be ready to receive benefits for not working. I felt I was way too young. Always the competitor, I have to win. Life never runs completely smooth, I saw my hip surgery as just one more obstacle thrown in my path.

Bad heart, bad hip, it didn't matter, I worked through it all. I thank my grandma again for instilling in me such uncanny work ethic. Hell, my bosses should have thanked her since I was their worker bee. I didn't believe in abusing sick time probably because I loved to be the one people could count on. Unlike some workers who had a tendency to be out for a nagging hangnail, I made it to work. I had the perfect excuse, but it wasn't in my nature to take advantage, and furthermore, I believe in karma. I didn't want a fake illness to come back and haunt me with a real one. I kept track of my own inventory, and knew there weren't any extra rewards for going back to work too soon or working while ailing. It was my thing, and I hoped others like my children picked up on it. Life was indeed good. I don't feel like a heart transplant patient that much anymore. In fact, my ten-year battle with heart failure now seems like "a pause for station identification... and now back to the show."

In the end when it's all said and done, my life will be determined by the greatest there is, and that's GOD himself. I've been sick for so long, and have caught a glimpse of the "other side," Therefore, major issues aren't so major anymore. I've learned to be more understanding of my body, and interpret slight ailments as warning signs of potential issues. What good is it to push your body to the brink of distinction when no one really cares? I have achieved balance between my mental and physical self. I refuse to be the guy in the casket who everyone says, "Wow, but he looks so good." The term "working yourself to death" is not part of my reservoir of clichés anymore. Yes, having a job is extremely important, but being able to live a healthy life trumps that every day.

Faith and Religion

I've found religion to be similar to politics. It's a very delicate and taboo subject, and many like me will quickly detour around the conversation. So many people try to force their religious beliefs down your throat, as if theirs are better than yours. My faith is strong, and got stronger as I leaned harder on the Man above when things were going all wrong.

People tend to get faith and religion totally confused. I have always kept my faith, but wouldn't consider myself the most religious person in the world. It's always been pretty astonishing how folks try to preach to you about going to church and finding GOD— always telling about what you should or shouldn't be doing. The funny thing is they're usually not the straightest arrows. I certainly understand people wanting to share their experiences, and how GOD has changed their situations. Do I really have to go to bible study and church every Sunday for GOD to give me blessings? Do

I really have to give a percentage of my salary to the church when my mortgage is behind, the refrigerator is bare and my kid's college tuition is due? My theory has always been: "Let me do me, and I'll let you do you." In other words, don't judge me and I won't judge you.

People get too caught up in keeping inventory of another person's house instead of making sure their own is in order. I truly don't have a problem with religious folks that pour their absolute all into the Lord. The *real* religious people are the ones that love GOD, and know that GOD loves all of his children, regardless of how many times they pray or go to church. Your beliefs, like politics, are your choice, unless you were a young boy in my household, and your grandmother was around. Now if this was the case, you'd be forced to attend Sunday school until you got old enough to make another choice—either get on the Sunday school bus, or play hooky with your brother and cousin until the two-hour service ended. Life gives us so many forks in the road.

Unfortunately, many of us reach out to GOD only in times of need, rather than simply to check in. I've been guilty of this myself. Since those early Sunday school days when the seed was planted, I've always had a sense of faith. I reached out during regular times, but most definitely I have called out as situations dictated. Obviously GOD's phone rang a little more frequently as my disease progressed. I admit I didn't always attend church, but have a great relationship with GOD. My belief has always been that you should believe in *something*. Mine happens to be my faith in GOD. He has brought me through incredible times when I thought I was doomed. People, perhaps nonbelievers, attribute everything to science and natural evolution, and may frown on this concept, but that is their choice. Believing in GOD has always worked for me. Like a prizefighter on the canvas, I was given the "standing eight count" on several occasions. Furthermore, I'm sure I could recall many other times He brought me through. I am compelled, however, to name some regarding the heart disease situation.

- One time while driving around a huge mountain, I became faint behind the wheel, but I was snapped back into consciousness. If I hadn't, I would have surely been maimed or severely injured due to my speed and the steepness of the slopes. It wasn't my time.
- On a particular night at work all alone and fainting, I was brought back after about nine seconds—according to the pacemaker reading. It wasn't my time.
- In my bathroom one early morning, fainting, with the defibrillator exhausting itself, I came through after forty-five seconds, albeit bloody and incontinent. It wasn't my time.
- Lying in the hospital for three months, waiting for the unfortunate passing of a donor so that I might live on through him, was further proof. It wasn't my time.

Another, one of my favorite sayings is "GOD is not done with me." These incidents prove this is true. I should have checked out many, many times, but my faith in GOD says He conquered the disease and the devil on so many occasions. So was that science, coincidence or the nature of the human body? Interpret that how you want to, but if my interpretation works for me, then who are you to knock it? I try to think intelligently, and not disrupt a person's belief. We all bear witness to the baseball player who continuously crosses himself, only to strikeout. I still don't question the fact that the next time up to bat, he uses the same approach, but this time hits a home run. That's the man's belief, and it works for him.

All I'm saying is: don't knock my faith. GOD works for me, and we have our relationship. Many times He's reminded me that He is my Savior, and I shall not want. Believe or don't believe, go to church or don't go to church, that is your choice. We all need to find something or someone in which to believe. I personally have the ultimate hook, and I've come to live my life by this saying: *Technology is great, but GOD is greater*. With each passing day, so many different medicines, inventions or procedures can give sick individuals a better quality of life. Even for people that have a grim prognosis, technology is constantly changing, giving newfound hope. I am clearly among the masses that love to hear about a breakthrough in medicine. Unfortunately, that wasn't always the case for a few of my loved ones and others in my life.

I was presented with the challenge of trying to convince my ex, Felicia, to never lose faith. She was stricken with ovarian cancer the same year I was in the hospital receiving my transplant. Before we knew it, the cancer reached Stage IV, and had spread to her brain. It was a clear and sunny day in May of 2011 when she told me it had spread, and the doctors gave her six months to live. I recall the day vividly because I was leaving the gym, sipping on a protein shake. I had no worries, and felt like I was on top of the world again. When Felicia hit me with the news, I was jolted back to reality. Cancer was taking a lot of people close to me, and I knew ovarian cancer in late stages was bad. Felicia asked me to tell our two boys, Jared, 21, and KJ, 27. Although Jared lived at home with her, I chose not to tell him her prognosis. It was a tough decision, but I wanted him to enjoy whatever time he had left with his mom. At that point, her doctors were suggesting hospice care, but I reminded her that GOD would determine her outcome. Felicia began to go to church more, and increase her prayers, as she became part of many prayer lists. I tried to help her by talking about my struggles and my faith. We shared many laughs along the way, as we did when were in our teens. She fought hard for herself and the kids, but cancer finally took this great woman on December 23, 2011. Only 47 years old, she was gone much too soon. My children were devastated. I was a mess as well. That could have been me. Her battle was a great one, but like my dad, and my boss, Tim, GOD had other plans for her.

I'm waiting on a miracle drug as well. It's hard to get a definitive answer to how long your new heart will last. When you're a transplant patient, it is only normal to have doubts—how long is my new lease on life? However, I believe that if you listen to others, read statistics or get caught up in a patient's misfortunes, you will be driven into a depressed or negative state. This is the reason why I focus on the second part of my phrase: GOD is greater.

My faith tells me that GOD has the final say in everything. Although I know I had one heck of a cardiac team making the right decisions, GOD guided all of those skilled professionals, including my talented surgeon. If I hadn't taken that mental approach, then I would have succumbed to this deadly disease a long time ago. Having said that, one has to be realistic as well, I diligently follow my doctors' orders. I eat a low-fat, low-cholesterol, low-sodium diet, and take my medicine as prescribed. I get proper rest, and I'm back to being the workout warrior.

True, you can follow all these parameters, and still get hit by a bus, but you have to put yourself in a position to resist the inevitable. Death is real. My faith tells me to live each day like it's your last, because tomorrow is truly not guaranteed. How many times in our lives have we heard about the untimely death of a young person or a seemingly physically fit individual? For me, this confirms it. When your number is up; your number is up. I understand that we should plan for the future, and set ourselves up for retirement, but I don't put as much stock in that concept anymore.

I'm trying to get my wife on board with my newfound ideology of living more for today. It's a tough sell for someone who has never peered through the squinted eyes of an ailing person. As in any marriage, I find the happy medium, and give her the "Yes dear." I would never let her think I was giving up early, but I live more in the "right now." We will plan for the future because my plan is to have one—but I know it really has more to do with GOD's plan.

Being sick for ten years battling heart failure, and then waiting for a transplant, had this affect on me. My life has become one cliché after another. The plan is simple "I'm going to ride the car till the wheels fall off." If my number comes up during the process, I'm okay because I know I lived life to the fullest. That is the message I want to leave. I've learned to not get caught up in worrying about things that are out of my control. I trust my doctors, but more importantly, I trust GOD. Every night and day I didn't pray to my surgeon, I prayed to GOD that He would bless me—*and* my surgical team. This is my faith because I believe my surgeon is a mortal, albeit a very talented mortal. I prayed that GOD would keep the surgeon's hands steady, and help him make quick, decisive moves. I even prayed a simple prayer that he would get a good night's sleep. I use the same prayer for pilots when I fly. At 40,000 feet in the air, I hope your faith is strong. Many don't believe in a higher power, and that's perfectly fine, but it's funny how many hypocrites I see at the slightest sign of turbulence saying, "Oh my GOD!"

It would be ludicrous for me to act as though a heart transplant hasn't produced a stronger faith in GOD. It has! I really don't sweat the small things. Although I don't go to church as much as I should, I still believe that GOD knows me as His child, and I can never fool Him. He knows what's in my heart, so I continue to serve Him in my way, and hopefully He will continue to bless me, and those around me.

To Donate or Not to Donate 24

No doubt that I'm a strong advocate for organ donation, but it's a bit surprising so many frown upon the concept. Whether I speak at naturalization and immunization ceremonies that introduce the donor process to citizens, or stand at the motor vehicles department, handing out donor materials, the results are often the same. Many people do not want to discuss the topic, and scurry away from me and the other volunteers. Like the saying goes, "Ignorance is bliss," and it's compounded by so much incorrect information about the subject.

When we don't totally understand something, we have a tendency to bypass it, especially if it doesn't pertain to us directly. I fell victim to this concept regarding politics. Although I was a bit younger, I felt politics didn't affect me directly, so I never gave it much thought. I've always known who our president and vice president were, but it was a never a source of major conversation in my household. In fact, I never heard my parents speak of voting. We actually learn many things in our homes when we're young, but as we get older, we can choose to start formulating our own opinions. It's a sure sign of maturity when we realize our parents don't always get it right. The right for African Americans to vote was amended in 1870, and was paramount in giving us equal rights. Eventually, I realized how important it was, and wanted to be part of the solution and not the problem.

I've come to witness the same change of perspective with organ donation. The people who are not affected directly are usually the folks who don't want to give it a thought. However, there are the many exceptions. It's all about education, and many of us are on the frontline helping to educate others. As recipients, we decided to not receive the gift of life—and then sit idly in the back. This includes my 13-year-old friend Laura who received her heart transplant a couple years back, and 52-year-old Rosanne who received the same. We're very proactive in pushing awareness.

Laura, along with her mom Jackie, has become a star player, and the two are everywhere promoting the value of organ donation. Many people can relate to her being a teen-ager, believing that if she's so animated about the topic, maybe it actually is important. Getting people to listen is the primary hurdle. Once we have their attention, the "sell" becomes relatively easy. What are we selling? Our product is a simple one, albeit a bit morbid. Here it goes:

"If something were to ever happen to you, GOD forbid, for instance a car crash, and you were to become brain dead, would you be willing to become an organ donor? This could possibly save the lives of as many as eight people."

A lot of times people won't let us finish the pitch because they fear the thought of dying. Before I took the time to really think about it—which is before I became ill—I didn't see it having a bearing on my life. I was totally ignorant, and I feel ashamed of myself because now I'm living proof of its value, and grateful my donor didn't think the way I once did.

People identify with Laura and her mom because everyone wants their child to have a chance to grow up. Laura speaks so well, is totally captivating, and is a great ball of energy. She has caught the attention of state senators as well, and they're trying to push along a new law. The law would state that through the Department of Motor Vehicles, all drivers would be donors unless they mark "no" or "not at this time." We all believe this would have the potential to greatly increase organ donations. People are always swayed by convenience, and how much easier could it be than to do nothing, while keeping two other options.

That new law would take a load off the many volunteers who like myself, stand outside the DMV trying to get people to sign up to become donors. I volunteer for this because I know the potential effect one single signee could have on saving someone's life, possibly that of a child. Our job there is tough because most of the people who go to DMV are in a rush, and have no time to listen. On top of that, we have to talk about the possibility of them dying? That's a bad combination, even for Laura. Here's a thought: Maybe I could hold my old heart in one hand, and take my shirt off to show passersby a transparent torso with my new heart. I'm sure if nothing else I could get a few people to stop to ask a few questions. It gets to be a bit embarrassing to get so many rejections. And besides, people can be downright rude. Volunteer duty is hard on the volunteer, but this is our fight to help spread awareness. At some point soon, another person like me, will eventually feel ashamed they didn't take the time to find out all there is to know about organ donation.

Rosanne is relatively new to the volunteer game, at least in my circle. I learned that I knew her brothers and her son. She can now be found everywhere from the Oprah show to hanging with Magic Johnson at organ donor walks. Rosanne is one of the few who actually has some interaction with her donor's family, and always carries a picture of her hero. This doesn't happen often, as the percentages are very high that recipients never get the chance to know their donor and family. It's natural for families to grieve, and they sometimes never get over a loved one's passing. Being on the receiving end, it's easier for me to say I would want to meet a recipient. Rosanne knows how lucky she is.

Ric, a college mate of mine, is a living donor. He made the incredible conscious decision to get his sister off dialysis by donating one of his kidneys to her. People like Ric are the definition of heroes. Imagine a person having no health problems at all who decides to give up one of his organs. It's a lot different than if you had an extra hundred bucks or even an extra car to give away. We're talking about a person deciding to have unnecessary surgery. Granted, most often it's done out of love, but the gift is so unimaginably generous. The living donor probably doesn't even ponder the thought of having the cushion of an extra kidney since the human body can function normally with only one.

You have people like Ric who donate to family members at their weakest moment, but there are also donors who step forward to help a total stranger. It's a little easier to comprehend the "Rics" of the world, but how those who come from a different part of the country to give up a perfectly healthy body part to someone they've never met? The word "honorable" doesn't seem to do this type of individual enough justice. Websites are now available to help the sick look for a willing participant who is a match. In the grocery stores when the cashier lobbies for an extra buck for "Susie's cancer treatment," I don't hesitate to say, "Sure I'll donate." I question my own integrity and willingness to donate an organ while I'm alive. I know I shouldn't, but I'm a realist. What if I gave a kidney away to the girl in Seattle, but later my child needed one? I would be so upset. I hold those living donors at the highest level of greatness. I'm sure GOD is going to have a special place set for them. In His kingdom.

Organ donation is gaining acceptance more and more each day. However, we still have a long way to go to get more people to understand it, and help others by registering to become a donor. I say: take everything I have because if I die, I won't need my body, as it is only a shell surrounding my soul. If I can save the life of another, until GOD calls that person home as well, then so be it. Why hoard your organs? We usually leave our money and other assets behind, right? Well, this is the same concept. Again, it's a "just-in-case" situation because people die everyday, taking their valuable organs with them. My new job is to educate people about the importance of donation. Simply put: I was going to die soon. Little Laura and Rosanne were about to perish as well. Three people (and their families) decided if something ever happened to them, then they wanted to help others. They saved our lives, and we carry the responsibility to not let them have died in vain. It's as simple as that.

I'm a messenger, and I want to scream to the world that organ donation/transplantation works. I pray for people not to be like me, but to be better than me. Don't wait for something to happen to you, your kid or another family member before educating yourself. I was lost but now I'm found. It's funny how GOD always has a plan for us.

Living with a Purpose

Random Statistics

2,332 heart transplants in U.S. 2011

72.4 percent are male

65.5 percent are white

19.4 percent are ages 35-49

54.2 percent are ages 50 or older

88.0 percent 1-year survival rate for males post-transplant

77.2 percent 1-year survival rate for females

79.3 percent 3-year survival rate for males

77.2 percent 3-year survival rate for females

73.1 percent 5-year survival rate for males

67.4 percent 5-year survival rate for females

9.1-year average survival rate of heart transplant patient

3,158 people currently waiting on a new heart

800,000 people worldwide need a heart

3,500 people worldwide on average have received a heart transplant

114,000 people in the U.S. currently are in need of a life-saving organ

8,127 deceased donated organs in 2011

6,669 living donated organs in 2011

90% say they support organ donation

30% know the essential steps to become a donor

18 people die each day waiting

So really, what does this all mean? This means that being too smart can kill you. I don't mean in the literal sense but there are many cases where people can't take grim news. Many times when you look for things, you sometimes find what you don't want to find. Diagnosed with restrictive cardiomyopathy in 2002, according to statistics, I should have been dead a long time ago. It was the stat that said most patients die within five years that startled me. I could have begun to hastily check off the remaining "to dos" on my bucket list, then taken the opportunity and killed myself. After reading that I could be dying within five years, I determined this was way Too Much Information (TMI). I may be going out on a limb here, but telling someone they may die soon could send them into a deep depression.

I learned a long time ago to not get caught up in statistics, For example, the weatherman on CBS says there's a 10 percent chance of rain, the NBC weatherman says 20 percent chance, and the ABC guy says 10 percent. After listening to this forecast, I detail my car for five hours, including a carwash, and then it pours. Yes, I now am most unhappy. Need another example? A baseball player can fail 70 percent of the time, and end up in the Hall of Fame. All he has to do is get three hits for every ten times he gets up to bat.

The statistics of women beating ovarian cancer is very low, so does that suggest it can't be done? Absolutely not, and I would have never suggested to Felicia to give up. There are always exceptions to the rule. Even though the current life expectancy of a heart transplant patient is close to ten years, should I soon start to make arrangements for my nonexistence? First of all, I would never concede to being average, and second, like I explained to Felicia, GOD has the final say.

So basically, I've come to believe that some statistics seem to be arbitrary, or used only for population studies. Many become a simple measuring stick. I researched so many facets of my illness, that although initial negative stats were shocking, I was able to eventually lessen the blow through my faith in GOD. I understand that if I know someone today who had a heart transplant thirty-one years ago, many people die during the first couple years after surgery to get the national average life expectancy down to 9.1 years. I believe in optimism. To believe that I'd be at the low end of that spectrum requires simply too much negative energy. I have to "aim for the fences!" If I happen to only hit the warning track, that's still a great shot. Translation: I'm going to live my life fully, and hope one day to die of old age. If something befalls me before then, it's something GOD intends. By living my life, I mean enjoying most things in moderation, especially if they're positive.

I refuse to look too far ahead because I'd hate to miss out on the little things right in front of me. Furthermore, most heart transplant patient's perspectives on the future are altered due to unknown factors. I have another person's organ in my body. How much more unknown can it get? I will do everything I can to extend my new gift's effectiveness. A healthy diet, along with exercise, no drugs, and limited alcohol intake, is a great start, but I will never be normal ever again. Normal people don't stop their morning gym workout at 9:55 a.m. to take a daily cocktail of anti-rejection drugs. I casually glance around the gym, and then inconspicuously, swallow my pills. My balance is off at times, but I understand this is my *new normal*. I deal with it and continue living.

As a fair-skinned African-American, I will always have to load up on sun block to avoid skin cancer. Cost-effective buffets, sushi, mushrooms, and medium-well steaks are now history in my life, due to possible bacteria. Normal people don't attend a 7:45 p.m. movie, and begin panicking at 9:30 p.m. because they haven't brought their 10:00 p.m. anti-rejection meds. They don't speed rush home, or meet their wife halfway, to make sure they take their medicine on time. No, the normalcy idea is out the window, but I will continue to look and act like regular folk. In my ten-year battle with heart failure, I learned to become a master manipulator and keep people from knowing how sick I was, but now, actually feeling like a new man, I realize how arduous that task was.

It's important to have people who have the ability to reach others talk about this subject of organ donation. I like to lead by example, so sometimes pitching how important it is, can be overwhelming because of my personality. However, I've decided to swallow my pride, and get on with the great message. This isn't a product that can sell itself like say, a luxury car. No, this is a life-or-death thing that needs an added push. My volunteer friends and I will continue to be rejected and ignored, but we won't give up because of our commitment to the donors who have given their lives for us. We believe being a donor can help the world. My kids, friends, and the rest of my family are now donors, because they finally understand what it's all about. That's what it really comes down to: knowledge. It is understandable that unfortunate things happen, and why not make a difference, when you can. If I could get away with not paying for car or life insurance, I would. But I don't because I prepare for the "just in case."

When my doctors joked about trading in a big problem for smaller problems, I had no idea what they meant. I now know. Sure, my new heart is the best addition to my body, but it does come with a small price. The medicines I take I'm sure are wreaking havoc on my kidneys and my damaged hip. At times I get headaches, rare prior to surgery, but probably due to my higher blood pressure. So I find it sort of humorous when people ask me how I'm feeling, and I reply "I'm great!" I'm not lying. I actually feel so much better now, in comparison to how I used to feel. I'm usually very upbeat with no real thought other than living my life. Only the occasional thought of my funeral saddens me because I have a hard time envisioning my family mourning me. I snap out of it because that's not for today. I'm back to getting compliments, about how I look, but I understand my body is simply a shell surrounding my soul. Death is inevitable, but I'm not wasting negative energy or bringing too much attention to it by constantly talking about it.

Life's good right now. Real good. I walk among the rest of the earthlings as I always have, and no one would know I've been transplanted unless I told them. I know I don't fit the mold of the average patient, although we come in all forms. It's very important to take care of myself physically, because it directly affects my mental attitude. I also know sick people might look at me and feel an uplifting sense of hope. I am sort of a poster child for heart transplant patients. As I speak to people on the waiting lists, it's important that they know that once given an organ, it's their responsibility to the donor, and to themselves, to take excellent care of the gift. Receiving the organ is a giant part of the process, but maintaining a healthy lifestyle is also significant.

The numbers are what the numbers are. These statistics indicate we have room for a lot of growth and increased knowledge about organ donation. We've got to do better. Of course, many people shy away from the topic. I did too, but unfortunately I didn't have anyone to grab my attention and help me understand the donor process. I've become part of the movement, and I'm willing to speak to anyone who will listen. I employ you to not be a "page turner" like I was about politics, I no longer quickly turn the page. Currently, we have a president I can actually relate to and I find very charismatic. I find myself reading more, watching news on T.V., and allowing my mind to expand, I know more about world news. That may not be popular with some people but it's something easy to comprehend. When we have something in common with a person or group, such as an illness or even political views, we tend to form a bond.

I was sick but now I'm not, and I hope people can relate to me. I believe this was part of GOD's plan. I've often been the "go-to guy" because I get it done. Letting the world know about organ donation is my new passion and calling, to let the world know that we can help bring a positive change to the numbers of donors and transplants. I will never tell someone what they should do, as far as donating, but what they could do. I want to instill the knowledge and facts of organ donation, and let people decide what they want to do for themselves. Personally, what could be more noble and human than to help save a life—if yours can't be saved? I'm a regular guy who did regular things, who, most likely, was born with a bad heart. I worked hard to keep my physical body fit, and though I didn't appear sick, I learned the hard way that looks can be deceiving.

Again, I purposely capitalized GOD the whole way through my book as a way of showing respect. This obviously means He is first in my life, and made my journey safe and successful. It's been an amazing ride. My incredible medical staff worked feverishly in order for me to receive this medical marvel. Yes, organ donation works. My plan is simple: to bring knowledge about donation to people that don't have a clue. Clearly it has worked for me.

Perhaps you remembered the Make-a- Wish trinket; I received from Nikki's co-worker. I guess my wish was predictable and I will let you in on the secret. On the small piece of paper I wrote: LORD, if it is your will, please bless me with a new healthy heart. I folded the paper and put it in the trinket. Weeks after the transplant, while sitting in my living room, I opened it. This will always serve as a reminder of how awesome GOD is.

A 21-year-old male from Ohio made a decision to become a donor in the event of his untimely death. I will be forever indebted to him and his family for bringing me back from the depths of hell, and saving my life. This young man had a plan, and I'm sure part of that plan was not to die at such a young age. But I'm blessed that his plan included being an organ donor. Although there's a song with the lyrics, "You're nobody until you die." my plan is to dispel that theory for as long as possible.

Memo to self: I will die. Until that day I will be too busy enjoying the new beautiful life I was given. To my loved ones; when that unfortunate time comes, don't cry for me, because I hope to be up in heaven hanging out with my donor who gave me a little more time on earth.

www.KelvinVsmithsr.com

Sources

United Network for Organ Sharing (UNOS)
Scientific Registry of Transplant Recipients (SRTR)
** (www.Buzzle.com/articles/heart-transplant-statistics.html)
Organ Procurement and Transplantation Network (OPTN)
New York Organ Donor Network (NYODN)

Save a life today

Sign up to be an organ
donor@ www.donatelife.net

Made in the USA
Middletown, DE
03 March 2015